WORD
PORTRAITS

WORD PORTRAITS

GREG HINNANT

CREATION HOUSE
A STRANG COMPANY

WORD PORTRAITS by Greg Hinnant
by Creation House
A Strang Company
600 Rinehart Road
Lake Mary, Florida 32746
www.creationhouse.com

Unless otherwise noted, all Scripture quotations are from *The New Scofield Study Bible*, authorized King James Version (New York: Oxford University Press, 1967).

Scripture quotations marked AMP are from the Amplified Bible. Old Testament copyright © 1965, 1987 by the Zondervan Corporation. The Amplified New Testament copyright © 1954, 1958, 1987 by the Lockman Foundation. Used by permission.

Scripture quotations marked NIV are from the Holy Bible, New International Version. Copyright © 1973, 1978, 1984, International Bible Society. Used by permission.

Scripture quotations marked NKJV are from the New King James Version of the Bible. Copyright © 1979, 1980, 1982 by Thomas Nelson, Inc., publishers. Used by permission.

Scripture quotations marked NLT are from the Holy Bible, New Living Translation, copyright © 1996. Used by permission of Tyndale House Publishers, Inc., Wheaton, IL 60189. All rights reserved.

Scripture quotations marked PHILLIPS are from *The New Testament in Modern English*, Revised Edition. Copyright © 1958, 1960, 1972 by J. B. Phillips. Macmillan Publishing Co. Used by permission.

Scripture quotations marked TLB are from The Living Bible. Copyright © 1971. Used by permission of Tyndale House Publishers, Inc., Wheaton, IL 60189. All rights reserved.

AUTHOR'S NOTE: In some of the Scripture quotations, with the exception of verses from the Amplified Bible, I have inserted in brackets explanatory text to help with the understanding of certain words. Also, any italics used in Scripture quotations are my own emphasis.

Cover design by Terry Clifton

Library of Congress Control Number: 2006933081
International Standard Book Number-10: 1-59979-087-4
International Standard Book Number-13: 978-1-59979-087-9

First Edition

07 08 09 10 11— 987654321
Printed in the United States of America

To believers everywhere who long to
become mature Christians—fully developed,
spiritually adult, consistently Christlike,
and a joy to their heavenly Father!

Acknowledgments

$\mathcal{I}$ wish to recognize and thank my dear, committed friends and associates at Greg Hinnant Ministries for their unflagging, selfless assistance and phenomenally faithful support. To Alice W. Bosworth, Jean Brock, Suzanne Hinnant, John J. "Jack" McHugh Jr., Virginia G. McHugh, Kathleen McHugh, Phyllis H. McNeill, Mary Ann Mowery, Chris D. Smith, Melissa N. Smith, and Evelyn A. Ward, let me say, God bless you, God reward you, and I love you!

Special thanks are also due to David and Deborah Garner for their kind help in orienting me to the ways and works of stoneware potters.

CONTENTS

PREFACE

W HAT IN THE world do stoneware pottery, eagles, salt, Oriental wise men, and ants have in common? Nothing really. Yet from a biblical perspective, these very dissimilar things have at least one significant similarity: they each tell us something about the *mature Christian*—who is fully developed, spiritually adult, and consistently Christlike.

The five word portraits in this book, though not lengthy, will nevertheless go a long way toward giving us an accurate concept of the end God wants us to reach in life. Before He sends His Son to take us to heaven, the heavenly Father has sent His Spirit to:

1. Make us *vessels of honor*, as a potter does clay
2. Teach us to fly over earthly difficulties in "the way of *an eagle* in the air"
3. Cause us to be the *salt of the earth*, filling us with the curative, valuable, and potent salt of Christ and training us to keep our savor strong
4. Make us *wise men and women*, teaching us the

wisdom of the Magi and guiding us in their ways
until we are in God's presence, worshiping

5. Expound to us the diligent ways of *the ant* until,
thoroughly embarrassed, we emulate the monumental wisdom of these minuscule creatures

And why should we let the Holy Spirit do these
things in us?

So that our characters may be conformed to the
image of Christ, which is the top priority on God's agenda
for Christians. If we study these five biblical "portraits,"
each of which teaches valuable lessons regarding the
character of the mature Christian, and if we practice what
we learn, we will one day emerge from the process conformed to the image of Jesus. He is the heavenly Father's
most honorable Vessel, the highest flying Eagle in heaven
and earth, the earth's mother lode of spiritual Salt, the
world's wisest Man, and its prime Workman, with antlike diligence. Indeed, *to be like Jesus*—"conformed to the
image of his Son" (Rom. 8:29)—is life's highest good and,
ultimately, the only goal worth pursuing.

To that end I write these words and offer this book.

—GREG HINNANT

Chapter One

MAKING VESSELS OF HONOR

He shall be a vessel unto honor, sanctified, and fit for
the master's use, and prepared unto every good work.
—2 TIMOTHY 2:21

A FEW YEARS AGO, and much to my surprise, the
Holy Spirit began creating in me a deep and growing interest in pottery. After stirring that interest by some
preliminary research and reading on the subject, I felt led
to follow the call of the prophet Jeremiah, to whom the
Lord said:

Arise, and go down to the potter's house, and there
I will cause thee to hear my words.
—JEREMIAH 18:2

So down to the potter's house I went, writer's pad and pen in hand.

> And when I arrived . . . Behold, he wrought a work on the wheels.
> —JEREMIAH 18:3

Unlike Jeremiah's experience, I did not visit a potter's house in the land of Israel. Instead, I visited one in the little town of Seagrove, North Carolina.

Situated squarely in the heartland of my native state, less than an hour's drive from my home, Seagrove is an internationally known haven for potters and their ancient art. Of the 275 total inhabitants of Seagrove, there are presently 117 potters—and counting! These remarkably gifted, financially courageous, and refreshingly free spirits make their living by practicing all kinds of potting methods and styles—stoneware, raku, crystalline, majolica, redware, earthenware, agateware, scraffitto, and so on. Their potteries are named as creatively as their pots: Dirt Works, Fat Beagle, Humble Mill, The Great White Oak Pottery, Whynot Pottery, Jugtown, Ole Fish House, to name a few.[1] Many Seagrove potters are native North Carolinians whose pot-crafting predecessors go back many generations (in some cases 200 years). But not all are provincials. Some have migrated from various parts of America to live and work in this quiet, distinctly off-the-beaten-path village, which many consider the unofficial pottery capital of the nation.

Seagrove is also home to the North Carolina Pottery Center, which is the first state pottery center in the nation and an excellent place to spend a few hours learning about pottery and feasting your eyes on the exquisite works of some the area's most talented clay crafters.[2] It was there that I was directed to one particular artisan, David B. Garner. A resident potter and proprietor of Turn and Burn Pottery, David is a fellow Christian.[3] He, along with his gracious wife, Deborah, made my day by providing me with all the technical information I needed concerning stoneware pottery and all the delicious Southern hospitality I could hold.

The exterior appearance of Turn and Burn Pottery doesn't begin to rival the architectural splendor of the Biltmore House, the nation's largest private residence, located a few hours' drive away in Asheville, North Carolina. Quite the opposite, its glory is not in outward appearance but hidden within its modest white-frame exterior and simple tin roof. Yet, once through the doorway, you immediately sense the obvious—*a potter is here!* Rows of simple shelves laden with all kinds of colorful earthworks—stoneware platters, cups, bowls, mugs, vases, pitchers, even birdhouses—betray both the master workman's proximity and productivity. So I went in to observe the potter, listen to his wisdom, and receive a word from the Lord. *How does he make these beautiful handcrafted vessels?* I first wondered and then asked.

So this artisan potter began to tell me. A devout believer who gives his time generously to evangelistic ministry in local prisons, Garner quickly disclosed that it is his "passion" for the art of pottery, not merely commercial interest, that has motivated him to design creations of clay for more than thirty years. He quickly added that every piece "begins with a vision," which he holds in his mind's eye. Before he begins each work, he knows exactly the end result he wants to create.

I learned that the prime requisite for creating fine pottery is good clay. Garner buys high-quality, specially blended potter's clay, free of roots, rocks, and other obstructions. He begins working with the clay by pressing and kneading it with his hands to eliminate air bubbles and distribute the moisture content evenly throughout each lump. After that process is complete, it's onto the wheel for the chosen lump of clay.

There, as the clay spins according to the potter's desire, he moistens it with water, which he applies periodically to his hands and fingers while applying pressure to transform the shapeless clay into the shape of the vessel he envisioned. "It's all touch," he assured me. During its dramatic season of change on the wheel, a lump of clay passes through many different shapes and sizes in a mystical and artful display of raw creativity in progress. If at this stage the potter is displeased with the formation of the clay, he simply reworks the soft, moist lump and begins turning and shaping it again. Once he sees the form he envisioned replicated before him, he ceases spinning the clay on the wheel.

Next, he carefully removes his work from the wheel and sets it on a large storage tray. After he wipes it clean, it will sit there, covered with a thin sheet of plastic paper, to dry gradually over the next ten days. This drying process must be controlled, Garner informed me, "to keep the loss percentage down." If a piece dries too quickly, its rim may develop a crack, which may later cause it to fail during firing. When the work is "leather hard," it is trimmed, and any desired attachments (for example, handles) are added. Also at this stage, the potter's "mark" is cut into the bottom side of the work. For many potters, that mark is their own simple but distinctive symbol, monogram, or logo. Garner prefers to use the ancient Christian symbol of a fish, his shop name and city, and a Bible verse. "It gives us a chance to share our faith," he explained. After being marked, each piece is again cleaned, returned to its tray, and left to finish drying. Once it is "bone dry," the clay is ready for its first trip to the oven. Among potters, this initial baptism by fire is called the *bisque firing*.

So into the kiln it goes, along with a host of other aspiring vessels of honor, to have its structural integrity tried and strengthened by a fiery ordeal. The bisque firing involves ten to twelve hours in a 1750 degrees Fahrenheit inferno. Such an all-encompassing, intense pressure will faithfully reveal if bad clay is masquerading as the right stuff. If there are flaws caused by moisture, air bubbles, rocks, or roots hidden in the clay, the fire will soon reveal it. How? It will "fail," or explode in the relentless heat of the kiln. And if it fails, it won't fail alone. In its exploding, it will damage or ruin many other vessels on every side, resulting in a sad, threefold loss: to itself, to its fellow vessels, and, most importantly, to the potter.

Once a bisque-fired vessel is cracked, it is literally good for nothing! Because it cannot be reground and made suitable for turning, it can never fulfill the potter's vision; nor can it, as a hard, half-formed piece of houseware, return fully to the ground from which it was extracted. If, however, vessels endure their initial fiery examination, their strength is greatly increased and their form made permanent. Now when water touches them, they will not lose their shape or return to the soft, impressionable clay of their origin.

Upon completion of this bisque firing, Garner leaves his kiln closed and lets his pieces cool in the same manner they were dried—very slowly, in this case twenty-four hours. This gradual, controlled cooling insures that his pieces will not crack due to sudden exposure to drafts of cool air. Once cooled, the pieces are again wiped clean to remove any extraneous matter (some potters sand their pieces at this stage) and placed on shelves to await the potter's next process.

That labor of love is the application of his *glaze*—a liquid (or powdered) substance of personally formulated colors (including clear finish) used to seal and decorate the work and give a distinctive glaze or *glassy* finish—to all surfaces except the underside. The potter's objective in glazing is primarily ornamental. He wants his pottery to be not only serviceable and durable but also beautiful. After the glaze is dipped, brushed, squirted, poured, daubed, or even sprayed onto the surface of a piece in one or more applications, it is allowed to dry for a brief period. Then it's ready for its final fiery trial, called *glaze firing*.

When committing his glazed works to the kiln, Garner refires them at 2400 degrees Fahrenheit for twelve hours. After his wood-fired kiln has reached temperature, he inserts a measured amount of moistened salt directly into the kiln. In the intense heat the salt vaporizes, pervades the kiln, and reacts chemically with the tiny particles of silica (sand) in the clay to create a glossy (high sheen) finish on his "salt-glazed" vessels. Glaze firing bonds the beauty (glaze) and the strength (bisque-fired clay) of the vessel into one permanently unified, useable work of art.

After the firing ceases, again, Garner seals his kiln to ensure a very slow, controlled period of cooling, usually for three days. Afterwards he uses very fine sand paper to rub off any burrs that may later scratch his buyers' fingers or furnishings. Then he gives each piece one final cleaning, wiping it thoroughly. And so there emerge from his house worthy vessels indeed, ready and able to fulfill three main purposes:

1. Function (usefulness)
2. Beauty
3. Honor

Regarding function, Garner's customers freely use his creative pieces however, whenever, and wherever they please. Some pottery serves as tableware, kitchenware, and other useful or decorative houseware. Other pieces, like his birdhouses, are used in outdoor settings.

Aesthetically pleasing, many of his works are displayed solely for their beauty. Many patrons place them on display in cabinets or on shelves, furnishings, or pedestals in their homes or offices. There they are enjoyed by others who appreciate the quality of their beauty.

As for the honor, well, that goes to David Garner, the artisan who envisioned and created each piece. He is blessed with a sense of satisfaction at a job well done every time some overly excited lover of pottery such as myself *oohs* and *aahs* at his handiwork. When we buy one or more pieces, Garner is blessed by the recognition of his God-given skills and rewarded for his faithful labors. From both his and his buyers' perspectives, his finished works are "vessel(s) unto honor" (2 Tim. 2:21).

ABOUT THE POTTER, HIS HOUSE, HIS WORK, AND HIS VESSELS

After returning home from the potter's house, the Lord showed me that what I had learned there was a biblical analogy illustrating some key spiritual truths about Himself, the *heavenly* Potter; His house(s), the universal and local church; His work, the transforming of our characters by the Holy Spirit; and His eternal vessels of honor, mature Christians. Let me share with you what He shared with me.

The Potter's patience

After being around David Garner for only a few moments, I couldn't help noticing his mild, soft-spoken manner and laid-back demeanor. This was not a man in a hurry. Shortly, his words confirmed my observations. "A potter has to be patient," he informed me, going on to explain that if a load of work is destroyed in the kiln, there's absolutely nothing he can do about it. When such unfortunate eventualities occur, he has learned to accept the fact that he has lost so many days or weeks of work and must simply start all over again. Also, if he is not completely satisfied with one of his glaze-fired products (because, for instance, it was in a "cool spot" in the kiln and therefore not sufficiently fired), he sometimes reglazes it, applying an additional adhesive mixture, and then refires it. A hasty potter would probably just chunk it and junk it. But Garner is not a hasty workman.

Nor is our heavenly Potter in a hurry with His work in our lives. Have we ever realized how enormously patient God is with us as He seeks to fully form the character of His Son in us? How many times has He quietly accepted it when we failed on the whirling wheel of life? Instead of throwing us back to the dirt yard of the world, He patiently began all over again, helping us to form basic Christian thought patterns, values, habits, and works. How many times have generations of Jews in Old Testament times as well as Christians in this Church Age miserably failed to do His will? Yet, instead of abandoning His vision for His covenant people, He has just quietly revived the next generation and called it to pursue the road to glory. We should praise and thank our heavenly Potter often for His marvelous, enduring patience!

The Potter's sovereignty

Supreme in his own workshop, Garner has truly godlike power over his clay. He can do literally anything he wants with it. He may make it into exquisitely decorated vases or simple bowls suitable for dog food. He may glaze it with bright colors or leave it unglazed. He may fire it in whatever kind of kiln (wood-fired, gas-fired, or electric) he chooses and however many times he wishes—once, twice, or even more. He may sell his finished product, warehouse it, use it himself, or give it away. He may put it in a special place of honor or smash it to pieces. Indeed, the destiny of each vessel is entirely in his hands.

The sovereign work of the heavenly Potter with believers is just as far-reaching. We can't do what we want to do with ourselves, because the Lord owns us: "What? Know ye not that . . . ye are not your own? For ye are bought with a price; therefore, glorify God in your body and in your spirit, which are God's" (1 Cor. 6:19–20). So don't ever try to resist the sovereign Potter. If He has you on His "wheel" of suddenly changing circumstances, don't strive against His will by despising your whirling situations. Don't rebel against Him by trying to change your circumstances without His permission just because you're uncomfortable, dizzy, or weary of "spinning."

Instead, be pliable. When the heavenly Potter's strong hands enclose you from both sides and press you upward, rise and stand upright and strong. When His thumbs gently rest on you, limiting your rise, humble yourself by fully accepting your subordinate position and limited authority in the home, workplace, or church. When His strong fingers press deep into your covetous nature, conform to His command to "be content with such things as ye have" (Heb. 13:5). Never make major decisions or changes in your life without first consulting and receiving guidance from the Potter; without Him, human clay can do nothing. "Apart from Me you can do nothing" (John 15:5, NAS). And when He clearly guides you, never question His wisdom; the way He leads is always ultimately best not only for the fulfillment of His will but also for your eternal benefit. "And we know that God causes everything to work together for the good of those who love God and are called according to his purpose for them (Rom. 8:28, NLT).

Because God redeemed you from Satan's power by the precious blood of His Son, He has every right to form your character as He wills to do what He wills, where He wills, when He wills, and with whom He wills: "Cannot I do with you as this potter? saith the LORD" (Jer. 18:6). If your spiritual progress seems slow, don't reproach yourself. Remember, you are a divine work in progress. To insult God's work is to insult God: "Shall the clay say to him that fashioneth it, What makest thou? Or thy work, He hath no hands?" (Isa. 45:9). And understand that, while He is patient, benevolent, and tender beyond description, your Potter is also capable of great wrath and awesome acts of judgment. If you stubbornly rebel against His transformation process, abandon Him, and persistently go your own way, He has every right (though no desire) to return you to the dirt yard from which you came. He may sell you into spiritual captivity to sin and its cruel master, Satan—or smash you in judgment, as He did Ananias and Sapphira. Why? Because the heavenly Potter is sovereign over all His works of clay. Wise vessels, therefore, learn to stand in awe of His supreme authority and power.

The Potter's passion

If David Garner, a redeemed son of Adam, is passionate about his creations of clay, how much more passionate is God, our Redeemer, about His eternal vessels?

To be precise, God is *super-passionate* about changing our characters into a spiritual facsimile, or more accurately, an authentic manifestation, of the indwelling noble character of Jesus Christ: "For whom he did foreknow, he also did predestinate to be conformed to the image of his Son" (Rom. 8:29). Daily God's heart yearns to form, turn, trim, clean, glaze, and fire our innermost being, that He may be honored in, and honor, us. Jesus encapsulated His Father's passion for our spiritual perfection (not sinless perfection but *spiritual maturity*, which is marked by the full development and consistent manifestation of the Christian graces, or "fruit of the Spirit," as Paul wrote about in Galatians 5:22–23) in His monumental command: "*Be ye, therefore, perfect*, even as your Father, who is in heaven, is perfect" (Matt. 5:48). By God's imparted grace and our consistent cooperation with His dealings with us, we may each grow into this biblical spiritual perfection—if we are passionate about it.

Do you share the heavenly Potter's passion for perfection? Or have you become indifferent about your spiritual development? Are you satisfied to just be "saved"—a useless lump of redeemed but unchanged clay in the house of God, bearing no resemblance to God or His Son? Or are you hungry to go on to fully know, fully obey, and fully glorify the One who saved you from a life of meaninglessness and an eternity of torment? Do you believe Jesus can really make you upright, noble, and spiritually minded? Or has unbelief robbed you of your vision of a truly sanctified life? Because many Christians do not aspire to or attain spiritual maturity does not mean that you cannot.

The heavenly Potter's Son shares His Father's passion. Two thousand years ago He stated in His message to the church at Laodicea (which, interpreted prophetically, also addresses this final "Laodicean," or grossly lukewarm and materialistic, period of the Church Age) that in these last days many of His Father's vessels would lose their passion for perfection and become spiritually and morally indifferent. He added that such halfhearted Christian vessels nauseate Him: "I know . . . that thou art neither cold nor hot. . . . So, then, because thou art lukewarm . . . *I will spew [lit. vomit] thee out of my mouth*" (Rev. 3:15–16). Hey, that's something for creatures of clay to think about. Do we want to sicken our Savior and be "spewed," or suddenly ejected, out of our place and work in His End-Time plan? That's the high price of spiritual passivity.

So see that you keep the Potter's passion alive and growing in your soul. Then, instead of increasing His and His Son's nausea, you'll help relieve it.

The Potter's vision

Because even the finest clay has no intelligence, it is powerless to strengthen, beautify, or improve itself to serve any useful purpose in this world. It needs a potter's vision to become something worthwhile or honorable. Only a potter can foresee the clay's potential in his hands. He alone has the intelligence to know how to fully realize that potential. He alone knows what the clay can become in His hands if it responds properly to Him.

Unlike clay, we Christians do possess intelligence. Yet, like clay, our intelligence is as nothing compared to that of our heavenly Potter. He said, "For my thoughts are not [as] your thoughts. . . . For as the heavens are higher than the earth, so are . . . my thoughts [higher] than your thoughts" (Isa. 55:8–9). Hence, the wiser we become, the less we will trust our earthly wisdom and the more we learn to depend on the Potter's heavenly intelligence to enable us to become something useful and pleasing to Him: "Trust in the LORD [His divine wisdom in all His guidance] with all thine heart, and lean not unto thine own [mere human] understanding [insight]" (Prov. 3:5). Before the world's creation, the Potter had a vision—an end conceived by divine intelligence—of what He would do in and through us in this life: "For we are his workmanship, created in Christ Jesus unto good works, which God hath before ordained that we should walk in them" (Eph. 2:10). That heavenly vision determines and motivates all God's dealings with us. Everything He allows to touch the soft, impressionable clay of our souls is sent to bring about a fulfillment of His original vision. If we are generally trusting and obedient, only one thing can hinder the Potter's plans: *other plans.*

Do you have your own plans for your life? "I have always wanted to try my hand at . . ." Are others trying to plan for you? "We really think you're perfectly suited to do this . . ." Are you blindly following the plans and paths that are popular in your generation without consulting the will of the heavenly Potter? "Everybody is doing things this way now, why don't you?" Or are you becoming wise and free enough to simply seek and follow the heavenly Potter's plans for your life? "Lord, what wilt *thou* have me to do?" (Acts 9:6). No matter how admirable, reasonable, alluring, popular, or successful other plans seem right now, they will prove worthless in the day of judgment if they were not God's plans for you. And if you follow them, He will declare you forever a vessel "to dishonor" (2 Tim. 2:20), and, though you will be saved, you will forever regret that you did not seek and serve His plan.

So earnestly seek and focus your heart on the Potter's vision for your life. Then follow it. Be whatever He wants you to be. Do whatever He wants you to do: "Whatsoever he saith unto you, do it" (John 2:5). Go wherever He wants you to go. Remain wherever He wants you to remain. And refuse to be distracted by any other plans for your life. Then you may look forward to the judgment seat of Christ and anticipate joyfully confessing there with the apostle Paul, and other vessels of honor, "I was not disobedient unto the heavenly vision" (Acts 26:19).

The Potter's instruments

As David Garner said, "It's all touch." However, his "touches" weren't always applied with his smooth, gentle, and forgiving fingers. Sometimes his fingers wielded less gracious instruments.

David's favorite instrument is his oft-used "rib," or wooden shaping chip. It is sharp and cuts mercilessly into the defenseless and highly impressionable clay. Universally, potters use a whole host of odd, little objects to cut (or "score"), trim, imprint, and sculpt their works. These instruments are invariably the simplest, everyday things, such as combs, can openers, lace (pressed into the clay, then removed to leave its pattern), rope, cooking utensils, credit cards, and so forth. All these small, hard, and imperfect objects help transform the soft clay into the perfect image of the potter's vision. I wonder if the clay knows that these mean little implements of vexation are held by the hand of a compassionate, wise, and visionary potter. Does it understand this, while the "flesh" of its surface is being painfully scraped, cut, imprinted, and molded to make it functional and beautiful—a vessel of honor? Probably not.

But we should. God wants us, His vessels, to be fully aware that He may use any kind of person, however sharp, hard, small, or odd, to shape us. As long as we are abiding close to Him by praying, worshiping, and seeking and obeying His Word daily, every person with whom we have contact is an instrument in the heavenly Potter's hand. He sends them to us and uses them to imprint, enlarge, and form our character as He has predestined it to be. But it doesn't happen automatically; we have to adopt the right attitude of submission in every situation.

The apostle Paul urged us to believe that God has a purpose in "everything" He permits to touch our lives: "In *everything* give thanks; for *this is the will of God* in Christ Jesus *concerning you*" (1 Thess. 5:18). A well-known proverb agrees that we should acknowledge God's control over not some but "all" our ways: "In *all* thy ways [circumstances] *acknowledge him* [the Lord's presence, hand, control, and hence, will]" (Prov. 3:6). This includes not only desirable but also undesirable situations; both are equally transforming in the Potter's creative hands. As we fully embrace the essence of these two scriptures—

which is *the attitude of acceptance*—the Spirit gradually turns, reshapes, and changes our outlook on every situation. We begin to realize that the Potter uses the ungracious actions of ungodly people to give us opportunities to respond in obedience to His Word and thus become more gracious and godly. While we have no control over their actions, we do have total control over our reactions. We can and must obey the biblical commands which they either do not know or are not willing to obey.

So if the "rib" that is impacting you presently is very sharp-tongued, haughty, hard, and unbending—a Nabal, Shimei, Zipporah, or Michal—don't be offended with the Potter. It's no accident. He sent that very human instrument—odd, broken, and perhaps manifestly diabolical—to change you, not vice versa. Though he (or she) may be selfish, unfair, and remorseless, in the Potter's hands that person is an instrument of your sanctification—the Potter's chosen means of making you magnanimous, fair, contrite, and compassionate as you walk in the light. So see them as such. Remember the Potter's high and holy purpose—to humble or soften *you*, to train *you* to forgive quickly, to be spiritually minded, and to please *Him* always. Yield and take the path the Bible calls you to take as your heavenly Potter removes more unwanted clay, or "flesh," from your personality. And it won't be the "rib" but you who will come away from the situation greatly improved—and on your way to distinction as a vessel of honor.

The Potter's house: a place of transformation

Turn and Burn Pottery is a house in which clay undergoes a process of radical change. From the moment it enters, fresh from the shipper's truck, to the day it leaves, a finished work of art caringly wrapped and bagged for the public, the clay is changing, developing, becoming.

It enters the potter's house colorless and useless and exits alive with color and reborn to a new purpose in life. It enters weak and leaves strong. It enters worthless and leaves valuable. It enters easily impressed by people and leaves as unchangeable as a rock. (Stoneware, the kind of pottery Garner produces, is so called because the intense firings return the clay to its original *stone-like* state.) It enters as common clay and exits as an uncommon and honorable work of art. It enters unattractive and leaves beautiful. Thus the potter's house is a place where clay experiences continuous and comprehensive transformation.

The heavenly Potter's house nearest you—your local church or assembly of believers, whether highly or loosely organized, whether attended by many or few—is also designed as a place in which clay is gradually but radically changed. Upon entering God's larger house (the body of Christ worldwide), we are frankly as ugly, worthless, common, weak, useless, and impressionable as a package of clay, albeit saved by the heavenly Potter's love and very dear to Him. We have entered His house and become members of His family by grace, as the songwriter put it, "Just as I am, without one plea."[4] Yet, God's plan is that we *not* remain as we are. Rather He seeks to thoroughly change us through the fellowship, ministries, and experiences, trying and triumphal, of our local assembly of believers.

There, in that smaller Potter's house, He alters us with Spirit-led teachings and sermons aimed at removing our rocks of hardness, roots of bitterness, and air bubbles of pride—unacceptable substances that, if left, would cause us to fail later in our fiery tests. There He challenges us by insightful pastoral counsel and frank mentorship that lovingly but directly exposes the faults in the clay of our characters. There He trims away our "flesh" (dependence on our old wisdom, strength, and ways) with the sharp, cutting edge of the sword of the Spirit, cleans us with the washing of the Word, shapes us by submission to pastoral authority, softens us by loving fellowship with other lumps of Christian clay, and firms us as we faithfully discharge small but God-given duties. Soon the transformation is becoming apparent: we are not yet a finished work, but we are no longer what we were.

We were weak, but now we're becoming strong. We were ugly with selfishness, but now the beauty of Jesus is becoming visible in our thinking, talking, and living. We were a useless lump of fallen human dust, but now we're a useful clay vessel in God's hands, ready to do His will, willing to wait patiently on the shelf or receive large amounts of living water and pour it out to bless, refresh, and sustain thirsty souls. This total willingness makes us valuable to the Potter, and honorable. Why? Because we have permitted His Spirit to change us.

Are we mindful of these things when we come to the house of God? Do we come to be changed or only to be comforted? To be enlarged or merely to be entertained?

To stay as we are or to become something we've never been? To remain wrapped in religious pride and self-will like most lumps of human clay or to be humbled by conviction, inspired by truth, and transformed by obedience into a soul valuable to God and man? These are the choices that are before us every time we enter the Potter's house.

The Potter's house: a place of many different vessels

One may find a world of different creations on Garner's shelves. His works come in all shapes: some thin and graceful and others slightly bulging in the middle. And they are many different sizes: some vases are nearly three feet tall, while some teacups are only two inches in height. They come in all colors: rich beige, pretty blue, soft white, dark brown, and black. Their "ages" are varied: some are fresh from the kiln, while others have been on the shelf for weeks. Like individuals, no two of Garner's creations are exactly alike, even those having the same design and glaze. Why? Because, as he emphasized to me, "They're handmade."

The church, or company of born-again believers in Jesus Christ worldwide, is precisely like the microcosm of clay creations in Garner's house. Believers come in all shapes: skinny, medium, and fat. And we come in different heights: some are seven feet tall, while others, vessels such as myself, stand about five feet, seven inches . . . with shoes on! We come in all colors: Asian yellow; Native American red; Hispanic, Middle Eastern, and Indian beige; African brown and black; and Caucasian white. Our ages also vary greatly: from children to adults to senior citizens. And our various ethnic cultures are too many to cite in this limited space. Yet even when our race, culture, and lifelong circumstances are the same, none of our personalities are exactly alike. The reason? We are all handmade, individually reformed in Christ by the invisible fingers of the heavenly Potter. Indeed, His house is a mini-world filled with *beautiful creations, beautifully different.* Obviously, then, He has no prejudices.

Nor should we. Do we deprecate and reject other vessels in God's house merely because their native clay is different from ours, or they are clustered on a different denominational or nondenominational "shelf," or their customs or order of worship differs from ours? Have we learned to appreciate and receive all of the Potter's clay creations with the same love with which He has received us? At Cornelius' house, Peter prophesied there would be a wide variety of vessels in the Potter's house: "Of a truth I perceive that *God is no respecter of persons*; but in *every nation* he that feareth him, and worketh righteousness, is accepted with him" (Acts 10:34–35). Speaking for the Potter, biblical writers declare no less than *seven* times that He is "no respecter of persons." (See Deuteronomy 10:17; 2 Chronicles 19:7; Acts 10:34–35; Romans 2:11; Ephesians 6:9; Colossians 3:25; 1 Peter 1:17.) Have we caught this, the Spirit's vision for the Potter's house?

The Potter's work: made of the right stuff

Potting clay is not just any kind of soil. Because their particles are too large, topsoil and field dirt are too porous to be used for pottery. Pure sand has no adhesion or stability at all and is therefore also unsuitable. Sandrock (shale), which is plentiful in my neighborhood, is too hard and dry to become a united, workable lump of clay. These and other kinds of earth matter can't be used to make fine stoneware. They just aren't the right stuff.

Quality clay contains very small particles of soil and is smooth, compacted, moist, and free of unwanted foreign elements (for example, rocks and roots) that would hinder the potter's handiwork on the wheel or cause it to fail in the kiln. Such clay is not the only prerequisite for success. As I mentioned, while working his pieces on the wheel, Garner moistens his fingers by periodically dipping them in water, which he keeps at hand. Thus his work's exterior surfaces are constantly moistened by small amounts of water from his fingers. Without this, his pieces would resist rather than respond to his touches. The essential importance of these simple materials—quality clay and water—cannot be overstated. Despite a potter's passion, vision, knowledge, artistic ability, diligence, and experience, he can do nothing unless he has the right stuff with which to work.

Similarly, despite God's consuming passion, clear vision, infinite wisdom, exquisite creativity, unflagging diligence, and vast experience in making vessels of honor, He can do virtually nothing with us until we receive the right stuff—the life and nature of His Son, Jesus Christ, and the baptism with the Holy Spirit—into our spirits. At the dawn of the Church Age the Potter's Son declared, "Ye must be born again" (John 3:7), thus mandating the new birth. When we repent of our sins and call on Jesus to save us, He forgives our sins and enters our hearts; thus we receive the quality clay of the kingdom, the righteous, holy, and loving nature of Jesus Christ, into our lives. But Jesus didn't just call us to be born again.

He also revealed the baptism with the Holy Spirit: "Ye shall be *baptized with the Holy Spirit*" (Acts 1:5). And He taught that this fuller anointing was necessary to · endue us with the power to walk and work with God in this godless world: "Ye shall receive *power*, after the Holy Spirit is come upon you" (v. 8). Not stopping there, Jesus personally baptized His original followers with the Holy Spirit on the Day of Pentecost. Only moments after that famous first infilling of "power from on high," Peter stood up and declared, "*He [Jesus]* hath shed forth this, which ye now see and hear" (Acts 2:33). So, like the new birth, the baptism with the Spirit is the chosen method of the heavenly Potter and the personal work of His Son.

Despite the richness and power of our initial baptism with the Spirit, the constant labors, stresses, and perils of this world make it necessary to receive fresh touches of the Holy Spirit—the Potter's "water"—every day to help us recognize and respond submissively to the Potter's dealings rather than resist them. Merely being baptized with the Holy Spirit will not make us vessels of honor; we must also obey the Spirit and do the simple things—waiting on God in prayer, worship, devotional reading, and Bible study—that enable us to receive regular refillings of the Spirit. (See Acts 4:31.) Then we are not merely Spirit-*baptized* Christians, or believers who were once filled with the Spirit but may have since quenched His flowing life and power (though He remains present). We are becoming Spirit-*filled* Christians, believers who daily practice the spiritual lifestyle that enables them to maintain the fullness of the Spirit. Without the moving of the Spirit in our lives daily, we often resist God's will just as dry clay resists the potter's touch. Why? We lack the right stuff. Finding what seemed to be the right stuff in Ephesus, the apostle Paul, who was one of the Potter's most skilled assistants, asked, "Have ye received the Holy Spirit since ye believed?" (Acts 19:2).

Well, have we? That is, do we have all the right stuff—the life of Jesus and the fullness of the Holy Spirit—in us? Are we receiving retouches and refillings of the heavenly Potter's "water" regularly by meditation in God's Word, prayer, praise and worship, and, most importantly, by obeying the Holy Spirit?

The Potter's work: turning

While there are other ways of making pottery, such as the "coil," "mold," or "slab" methods, most of Garner's works are "turned," or created while spinning on his electric, variable-speed potter's wheel. While on the wheel his works are constantly turning. Garner, not his clay, determines when and how fast the revolutions come and when they stop. To the clay, this perpetual motion makes life seem fast, furious, and out of control. But Garner understands that his work is not spinning wildly. With ever-watchful eyes and steady hands, he keeps it perfectly under his control at all times.

Similarly, the heavenly Potter personally controls every phase of our lives daily, always working all things together for the ultimate good of those who obey and follow Him (Rom. 8:28). He turns us on His wheel of circumstance, when and at the speed He wills, by initiating changes in our friends, associates, churches, jobs, schools, and neighbors, or by sending other unexpected situations our way. Every one of these divinely controlled "turnings" is sent to change us. Just as clay assumes many different appearances as it turns on the wheel, so God intends that our attitudes and living habits undergo many different changes as we learn to obey His Word and pursue His will in the different settings and among the different people He brings. We sometimes fail to fully realize that God is controlling our whirling circumstances, because they seem to change randomly, sometimes at what we think are the worst possible moments.

But no matter how unsettling and disruptive they seem, a Christian's circumstances are not accidental but providential: "*In everything . . . this is the will of God* in Christ Jesus concerning you" (1 Thess 5:18). While the clay is on an earthly potter's wheel, everything that touches it is part of the potter's plan. As believers, our peace comes in realizing that everything out of our control is still within the heavenly Potter's control. He assured His troubled lump of clay, King Rehoboam, "This thing is from me" (1 Kings 12:24), and Rehoboam quickly accepted an otherwise unacceptable situation. The quicker we accept our Potter's sudden turnings, the quicker our characters are shaped by His invisible hand and the sooner He takes us on to the next phase of His work.

So, "my brethren, count it all joy when you fall into various trials" (James 1:2)—that is, when the Potter turns you *again* just when you had hoped to stop spinning and enjoy peace and quiet. No matter how wild and chaotic, your times are surely, and securely, in His hands: "My times are in thy hand" (Ps. 31:15).

The Potter's work: cleaning

David Garner cleans his clay creations often: once after they are turned, again after they are bisque-fired, and finally, after they are glaze-fired and sanded. He is obviously aware that unclean works are not useful, beautiful, or honorable. Nor will they sell. Who wants to buy a piece of smudged pottery? Who would dare put it in a place of honor?

Similarly, the heavenly Potter is ever intent on cleaning us, His vessels. Time and again He washes us with His Word as anointed instructors teach us: "Now ye are clean through the word which I have spoken unto you" (John 15:3). The Word itself also cleans us every time we obey it: "Seeing that ye have purified your souls in obeying the truth" (1 Pet. 1:22). The Potter also cleanses us whenever, convicted by His Spirit or pressed by His chastisements, we humbly confess and forsake our sins and faults: "If we confess our sins, he is faithful and just to forgive us our sins, and to cleanse us from all unrighteousness" (1 John 1:9). And He purifies us when, to avoid harmful despiritualizing influences, we break off close relationships with unbelievers or sinning Christians: "Be ye not unequally yoked together with unbelievers" (2 Cor. 6:14). "Neither be partaker of other men's sins; keep thyself pure [clean]" (1 Tim. 5:22). In these ways His invisible hand wipes away the remnants of our old life, such as carnal reasoning, worldly desires, sinful behavior, bad habits, and un-Christlike attitudes. As a result we become increasingly sanctified—or holy, set apart exclusively for God and His use—and obedient to the apostle Peter's charge: "As he who hath called you is holy, *so be ye holy* in all manner of life" (1 Pet. 1:15).

This divine cleansing—by receiving teaching, reading the Word devotionally and obeying it, confessing our sins, separating from sinners, and so forth—serves three worthy purposes. First, when our cleansing from sin is deep and real, we honor the heavenly Potter, the Holy One, who has cleansed us. Second, people are then drawn to Him and His Son through us: "No man can come unto me, except the Father, who hath sent me, draw him" (John 6:44). Sinners are not drawn to carnal Christians; they are already well acquainted with uncleanness. But true holiness, a rare find in this world, fascinates and attracts them. Third, the heavenly Potter will use every vessel that submits to His cleansing process—but no others. While He stands ready to cleanse and use any of us, however defiled, He will never use stubbornly impenitent dirty vessels. Why? Because He is uncompromisingly holy. The apostle Paul urges us to be clean and be used: "If a man, therefore, purge himself . . . he shall be a vessel unto honor, *sanctified, and fit for the master's use*" (2 Tim. 2:21). Are we keeping our vessels clean, inside and out, and "fit for the master's use"?

If not, "let us cleanse ourselves from all filthiness of the flesh and spirit, perfecting holiness in the fear of God" (2 Cor. 7:1).

The Potter's work: waiting

While visiting Turn and Burn Pottery, I soon learned that the potter wasn't the only one who was patient. His clay creations also had to wait. (Bear with me, please, as I assign consciousness and free will to these inanimate objects.) Indeed, waiting was an essential part of the drying and cooling phases of their formation. In Garner's back rooms I saw many rows of recently turned or bisque-fired works sitting quietly and submissively on trays or shelves awaiting their next visit from their maker. Had they evaded these waiting periods, they would only have ensured their own demise. Without waiting until they were bone dry, for instance, newly turned pieces would fail during firing. Or, if after being bisque-fired they refused to gradually cool in the kiln, they may have cracked if suddenly exposed to drafts of cool air. In either case, impatience would have ruined them, leaving them unusable, unbeautiful, and dishonorable. How wise they were, then, to wait patiently for the potter's next work.

Have you, my fellow work of clay, learned the profound wisdom of waiting for the heavenly Potter's next work? If He puts you on a shelf for a season, accept it. Let all the things of your past life—the pride of life, the lust of the eyes, and the lusts of the flesh—dry up and die, until only the pure clay of the Christ-life is left. Then you'll be able to stand any fire. If the Potter releases you from a fiery personal conflict or red-hot season of ministry into a cooling period of quiet routine and unheralded duty, accept it. You need time to settle down, reflect on the lessons learned in the fire, and prepare for your next challenge. So "be content with such things as ye have" (Heb. 13:5) and practice the wisdom of waiting. "Let patience have her perfect work" (James 1:4). Know that you are only as perfect as you are patient and that impatience is imperfection manifesting itself.

When the Potter is ready, He'll visit you and move you to a new place of service. In that new season, you'll neither crack in fiery trials nor fail in your service, but you will stand strong and useful, a finished, honorable vessel without any defects. Truly, "you will be ready for anything, strong in character, full and complete" (James 1:4, TLB).

The Potter's work: attachments and trimmings

When I first arrived at the potter's house, Garner was attaching handles to some leather-hard mugs. After "scoring" the mugs (a few shallow, parallel incisions) exactly where he planned to join the handles and applying "slip" (liquified clay used for bonding) to these points, he attached the handles of fresh clay, gently forming the desired curvature and pressing the soft ends of the handles to merge smoothly with the leather-hard body of the mugs. By doing this he joined the two separate creations into one united work.

Garner also does his trim work at this leather-hard stage. For example, he places his bowls upside down on his wheel and, while turning them, cuts off unwanted clay to sculpt a circular, symmetrical base that is both strong and graceful. At this point his work, though still unfired, is fully formed.

Has the heavenly Potter "attached" anyone to you? Has He brought into your life another Christian friend of equal faith and commitment? Has He added a godly wife or husband, or children who have become serious about walking closely with Him? Or has He "attached" you to a teacher, evangelist, missionary, or church in order that your gifts of helps or administration may facilitate more sowing of His precious seed? Has He brought you under the tutelage of a wise and loving spiritual mentor so that you too may become wise and loving and fully formed in Christ?

Sometimes He brings two or more ministers together for specific works: "Separate me Barnabas and Saul for the work unto which I have called them" (Acts 13:2). (See also Exodus 4:16, 27; Ecclesiastes 4:9–12.) The Potter's Son first called (Luke 6:13–16) and later commissioned (Mark 6:7) His original disciples in pairs. Whenever the Potter attaches another work of clay to you, be faithful to that divinely ordered union. Fulfill your end of the relationship joyfully, to please the Potter, whether by teaching or learning, praying or assisting, exhorting or fellowshiping, giving or laboring, and let neither people nor demons put asunder what God has brought together. The Potter also "trims" His work in our lives.

He "trimmed" Abraham several times. He first cut away Abraham's hometown and country, Ur of the Chaldees. Then He removed his father, Terah, when he died. Next He removed his worldly nephew, Lot, when he chose to reside in Sodom. And finally, He removed Abraham's wife, Hagar, and son of the flesh, Ishmael, by ordering the patriarch to send them away. Every time he experienced these painful but necessary "circumcisions," or trimmings of various remnants of the old life, Abraham quickly accepted them and grew more gracious and strong in the faith.

When the Potter "trims" you by decisions, actions, and occurrences beyond your control, follow Abraham's example and accept it quickly. Don't try to hold to uncommitted Christians (spiritual parasites), unspiritual pastimes, or distracting interests or responsibilities once He intervenes to remove them from your life. Release the "clay" that will not or cannot be a part of the Potter's plan for you, a vessel He is developing for honor! Decide and pray, "Thy will, not mine, be done!" If you don't, you will hinder your formation as an honorable vessel or make yourself unfit for the Potter's service. The apostle Paul noted that we cannot be vessels of honor while we are closely associated with vessels unto dishonor: "If a man, therefore, purge himself from these [vessels "to dishonor," v. 20], he shall be a vessel unto honor, sanctified, and fit for the master's use" (2 Tim. 2:21).

The Potter's work: glazing

After his bisque-fired pieces finish cooling, Garner applies one of his personally formulated glazes to them. These coatings of vibrant, beautiful colors make his vessels as beautiful as they are strong and very appealing to buyers.

Just like the potters of Seagrove, the heavenly Potter develops His own glaze. But, unlike them, He only uses one unique glaze to coat the redeemed sons of Adam— the colorful and shining beauty of His Son. The psalmist calls this glaze, "the beauty of the Lord," and expresses the

Potter's will perfectly in his prayer, "Let *the beauty of the* LORD our God be *upon us*" (Ps. 90:17). In this age, that beauty was initially seen upon the Potter's first and most-prized vessel unto honor, Jesus of Nazareth.

When it was exhibited among men, His beautiful character and gracious personality attracted multitudes to receive Him. Envious, Jesus' worst enemies were forced to admit how attractive He was: "The Phari-sees . . . said . . . Behold, the world is gone after him" (John 12:19). To this day honest secular historians must admit, however reluctantly, that Jesus was, and still is, the most fascinating personality in world history. Even avowed atheists and agnostics are left gazing, wonder-ing, and permanently impressed at the loveliness of His personality, life, and works. One New Testament epistle calls the Potter's glaze "the fruit of the Spirit": "*The fruit of the Spirit* is love, joy, peace, long-suffering, gentleness, goodness, faith, meekness, self-control" (Gal. 5:22–23). These nine different "fruit" produced by the Spirit's pres-ence reveal the various shades and hues of color contained in the Potter's glaze. And the good news is, as we abide near to the heavenly Potter daily, He increasingly glazes our personalities, until "the beauty of the Lord our God" is seen upon us.

It is this glazing of Christ, this mystical, inter-nally wrought but externally visible work of divine art-istry, that attracts others to the heavenly Potter through us. Like buyers browsing through a potter's shop, peo-ple live life in this world endlessly comparing, consci-ously or unconsciously, the various human vessels they meet. When they see the rare, beautiful colors of the

Christ-life upon us—love, joy, peace, long-suffering, gentleness, goodness, faith, meekness, self-control—they first wonder: "Now when they saw the boldness [unshakable confidence of faith] of Peter and John . . . they marveled . . ." (Acts 4:13). Then they attribute the exceptional grace to the exceptionally gracious One with whom we have been closely associated: ". . . and they took knowledge of them, that they had been with Jesus" (v. 13). Soon afterwards a kind of spiritual "sale" occurs. Inwardly they decide, "I want *that* life in my life." Its purchase price having being paid in full by another, they receive the free gift of salvation through accepting the Potter's Son into their hearts.

To receive glazing, a vessel must be so near to its potter that his hand may hold it while he applies his glaze. Are we abiding closely to the heavenly Potter, so that He may rest His supernaturally creative hand upon us? Is He glazing us more and more with the beauty of Jesus? The glaze of His character must be "lifted up," or clearly seen in our lives, for the Holy Spirit to draw others to the Potter's Son through us: "And I, if I be lifted up . . . will draw all men unto me" (John 12:32). Shouldn't we, therefore, pray this paraphrased version of the psalmist's prayer? "O heavenly Potter, hold me close to You and finish glazing Your Spirit's work in my life. *May the beauty of the Lord be seen upon me!*"

The Potter's work: firing

Once the glaze has dried, it's time again for the "ministry" of fire. Garner's initial bisque-firing establishes the strength, form, and integrity of his pieces. If any bad clay is present in a piece, it will crack or explode during its first firing. The "glaze-firing," which is the final test of the potter's work, serves several vital purposes.

First, it makes permanent all the work he has put into his pieces—turning, trimming, attaching, cleaning, and glazing. After this final firing, his pieces are permanently established; their internal substance and external appearance never again change. Second, it gives him confidence in his pieces. He knows that after passing through the fire *twice* they are fully tested and proven and will never fail in any normal usage. They have no hidden faults. Hence, he may use or sell them without any misgivings. They are tested vessels ready to faithfully serve their buyers. Third, firing prepares his vessels for service in extreme conditions. No matter how much water they are immersed in, they will retain their shape and not revert to useless clay. And if they encounter great heat or have heavy pressure placed upon them, they will not explode, crack, or collapse. In a word, they are perfect: strong as a rock, beautiful as a gem, tested by fiery pressure, and ready for use.

What a fitting description for mature Christians! God wants us to become just like Seagrove stoneware: strong as stone, beautifully gracious, proven, reliable, and ready. His plan is that our fallen clay return to the rock-solid strength the Potter originally intended for mankind before the Fall and that the beauty of Christ, His perfect man, cover us from head to foot. And He has the sovereign power, passion, and patience to do this in us, too, if we don't fail in the fire.

The Potter's work: failure in the fire

Occasionally even the best potters' works will fail in the kiln. Why? Because something wasn't as it should have been. Something wasn't according to the potter's plan or in his order. Usually, the culprit is bad clay.

Like blazing kilns, fiery trials invariably expose any "bad clay" remaining in our lives. Intense, pressurized personality conflicts, overheated enemies, caustic criticisms, incendiary controversies, inflammatory rumors, burning rejections, long, hot summers of waiting—when these consuming pressures envelop us like a fiery oven, it becomes impossible for our spiritual faults to remain undetected. Rocks of self-will and stubbornness; bitter roots of covetousness, envy, or unforgiveness; air pockets of pride, anger, and impatience; the moisture of worldly ambitions, fleshly lusts, and secret sins; and the cracked edges of shallow or false teachings—the fire forces all these to manifest: "Every man's work shall be made *manifest*; for *the day [of testing] shall declare [reveal] it*, because it shall be *revealed by fire*; and the fire shall test every man's work of what sort it is" (1 Cor. 3:13). The moment we recognize these faults within us is the moment of truth.

If we confess and forsake them, God graciously removes them, and we continue progressing toward spiritual maturity: "If we confess our sins, he is faithful and just to forgive us our sins, and to cleanse us from all unrighteousness" (1 John 1:9). But if we deny them, they will remain and eventually cause us to fail, or *explode*, in the kiln of testing. Our faith will not merely lapse but suddenly and catastrophically collapse. We will not briefly stumble and recover ourselves but permanently, openly *rebel* against the Lord and everything we associate with Him—including His Word, ways, and church, the people to whom He has attached us, and our duties or ministries—and, as an apostate, return to our old sins, associations, and ways of living.

It would be tragic enough if failing Christians just quietly and neatly imploded, leaving other vessels and observers unaffected. But that never happens. If we explode in the fire, other souls, especially those nearest and dearest, are always profoundly harmed as they see our faith go to pieces. When Christian vessels fail, observers usually blame the Potter, assuming that somehow He failed them, that His Word is errant, His Spirit impotent, His Son a fraud, and His people foolish. Failure in the fire results in a tragic threefold loss.

First, we lose the pure joy of being honored and used by the Potter, who cannot and will not use failed (stubbornly unsanctified or apostate) disciples, and forfeit part or all of our eternal rewards in Christ. Second, others lose because they will never see the beauty of the Potter's Son in our lives and be drawn to Him. Third, the Potter loses, because He will never be fully satisfied with us as His servants or receive honor for having finished His work in our lives; thus we diminish His joy and glory in our lives.

Despite this perilous possibility of failure in the kiln, potters still require that all their pieces endure the fire—not once, but twice. Why? Because they know that without firing, their pieces can't be finished.

Nor can we. Have we fully grasped the basic lesson revealed by the potter's work, namely, that while bad clay can't survive the fire, good clay can't be made into honorable vessels without it. In short, this tells us that *while carnality can't survive fiery trials, mature spirituality can't emerge without them.* We simply can't be finished vessels unto honor unless we pass through the fire! Without it we would be as soft and weak as unfired clay. At the first touch of troubled waters, we would melt with fear and compromise, or we would shamefully abandon God's Word and calling in our lives. If God should place heavy responsibilities upon us, we would crumble under the load and draw back rather than press into His will. And the heavenly Potter's glaze, the beauty of His Son, would never bond to us. We would remain as we were: saved by God's grace, but weak and unbeautiful.

So let's make peace with our blazing kilns. We need their ministry of fire! Rather than despise fiery tests, let's embrace them with contentment: "I have learned, in whatever state I am, in this to be content" (Phil. 4:11). And to ensure our spiritual growth, let's rejoice in the midst of our kilns: "Beloved, think it not strange concerning the fiery trial which is to test you, as though some strange thing happened unto you, *but rejoice . . .*" (1 Pet. 4:12–13). (See also 1 Peter 1:6–7; Daniel 3:25.)

The Potter's work: with salt

Many Seagrove potters, including Garner, insert a large amount of moistened salt directly into their kilns during glaze firings to give their pottery a glossy finish. The *salt-glazed* pieces that emerge are not only strong, proven, and beautiful, but they also shine.

Similarly, God wants His vessels to not only be strong and winsome but also to shine with the radiance of Jesus. To this end, He seeks to add the salt of gracious speech to us while we're in the fiery trials of life. How? His Spirit persistently deals with us to yield our tongues to Him and speak as a vessel of honor: "Let your speech be always *with grace*, seasoned *with salt*" (Col. 4:6). No small task, this mastery of our tongue is one of the last graces to be perfected in us. In the intense pressures of our final trials of Christian maturity—hotter kilns than any we experienced earlier in our walk—we soon realize that it is imperative that we learn to speak the truth in love. Too much damage—angry contention, confusion, turmoil, bitterness, emotional harm, and permanently lost opportunities—results when we don't. We must not only be right, but we must also speak rightly.

Salty speech is beautifully balanced. Those who have it are bold, but not insolent; firm, but not harsh; frank, yet kind; confident, but not proud or arrogant; winsome, but never insincere or misleading. They are discreet, discerning when to be silent and when to speak; when to limit their response to a simple *yes* or *no* (Matt. 5:37) and when to offer further explanations to ensure understanding. Not contentious, they disagree without being disagreeable. And they remember the command, "The servant of the Lord must not strive [hotly contend or argue]" (2 Tim. 2:24). Humbly, they quickly retract all unkind, disrespectful, or inaccurate statements. Daily they seek to be "swift to hear, slow to speak, slow to wrath" (James 1:19), knowing that "the wrath of man worketh not the righteousness of God" (v. 20). In short, they aspire to speak with the graciousness of the Potter's Son.

Of the Potter's Son it was said, "Never man spoke like this man" (John 7:46). The heavenly Potter wants to manifest the same graciousness in our conversation. He did so in Stephen: "And they were not able to resist the wisdom and the Spirit by which he spoke" (Acts 6:10). He did so in Martin Luther, who gave admirably gracious testimony before the Diet of Worms. He did so in William Tyndale, whose flowing prose translations of the original Hebrew and Greek Scriptures comprise approximately 90 percent of the Pentateuch and New Testament in the Authorized Version of the Bible (KJV). He did so in Charles H. Spurgeon, whose sermons and books are of singular spiritual quality and eloquence. He did so in Billy Graham, whose regal voice heralded the Christian evangel throughout the world for decades with Christlike grace. He has done so in many thousands, perhaps millions, of unknown Christians who have walked humbly with Him in times past. And He stands ready to do the same in us today.

The more we let the Potter have His way with our tongues, the more "perfect" (spiritually mature) His work will become in our lives: "If any man offend not in word, the same is a perfect man" (James 3:2). And the more spiritually mature we are, the more our words will shine with the radiant and winsome grace of the Potter's Son.

The Potter's vessels: without offense

After Garner glaze fires his works of pottery, he uses fine sandpaper to ensure that all their surfaces, especially their bases, are smooth. Why? He doesn't want his pieces scratching his customers' furnishings or pricking their fingers. That would be inexcusable and offensive. A wise merchant, Garner wants his vessels to be without offense. His chosen means to this end—sandpaper—is ineffective unless it directly contacts a piece of pottery and *rubs against it*. Though it creates undesirable discomfort, this abrasion also achieves the potter's desire—the parts of his pottery that offer resistance are worn down until they no longer exist, leaving them smooth and inoffensive.

Similarly, there are times when God uses human sandpaper—strong-willed, rude, rough, mean, hard, cold, arrogant, unfair, or vengeful people—to finish the work of His Spirit in our characters. He used Nabal to help finish His work in King David's life. (See 1 Samuel 25.) First, David contacted Nabal by sending his messengers to request help. Nabal in turn made coarse, cutting comments to David, and friction ensued, as David immediately began resisting Nabal's evil words. But when Abigail gave David God's wise counsel, he yielded to the word of the Lord and stopped resisting his arrogant accuser. Thus God used the abrasive actions of an unworthy vessel to remove one of the last burrs of carnal resistance—the pride and strife of self-vindication—from His vessel of honor. And David emerged a perfectly inoffensive man.

God wants to do the same with us today. He brings abrasive people around us and allows their attitudes, actions, and words to rub us wrong. Friction and heat quickly build in our minds as we think about how unfair or unloving they have been. Then the Holy Spirit brings to mind the Word of God that applies to the situation we face: "Fret not thyself because of evildoers." "Cease from anger." "Resist not evil." "Avenge not yourselves." "Commit your way to the Lord." "In everything give thanks." Always His counsel addresses what *we*, not others, should do. As we yield to and obey God's Word—not resisting evil but forgiving, not grudging but forsaking anger, not retaliating but overcoming evil with good, not seeking vengeance but forsaking it, not arguing with but praying for those who misjudge us— the nicks and burrs from our old spirit of carnal resistance are removed. Every time we take the humble line of simply *pleasing Jesus*, the Spirit of God sands off more of our rough attitudes, sharp words, and offensive mannerisms. Our new, more humble, nonretaliatory attitude renders us sociably smooth, finished vessels—Christians with whom it is easy to live, work, and minister. And we emerge from the Potter's house as inoffensive, spiritually mature Christians.

Even so, people may occasionally *take* offense with us if they dislike the Potter's Son, His Word, or His high standards of righteousness, which we unobtrusively yet unashamedly embrace, confess, live by, and teach. But we can't avoid this; all who despise our Master will despise us, too. This is our honor, not our dishonor: "If any man suffer as a Christian, let him not be ashamed, but let him glorify [praise, thank, worship] God on this behalf " (1 Pet. 4:16). In cases when we are rejected for Christ's sake, we are not guilty of *giving* offense. We are only guilty when we fail to obey the Potter in what we say or do while interacting with people. On those occasions we should ask forgiveness of those whom we have offended, as Jesus taught us (Matt. 5:23–24), so that we may receive forgiveness from Him.

The Potter's vessels: durable, useful, beautiful, honorable

Once finished, Garner's pieces are durable, useful, beautiful, and honorable. Firing has made them strong and durable. Stoneware lasts for centuries—virtually forever. As stated earlier, his pieces are widely used as serving trays, tea kettles and cups, coffee mugs, fruit bowls, plates, platters, wall ornaments, vases, and even birdhouses. Their beautiful glazes make them both pleasing and attractive to the buyer's eye. And every clay creation brings honor to its creator. One admirer of Garner's works tells another, who tells another. As his reputation grows, more people are drawn to his house, to his lovely vessels, and to him.

Similarly, the heavenly Potter's handiwork in our souls makes us as durable, useful, beautiful, and honorable as fine stoneware. Our proper response in our fiery trials makes us enduring servants of God. That we have already passed through intense tests without failing prompts God to call on us confidently for difficult assignments. He knows we will endure to the end, because we have done it before. Just as stoneware serves human kind indefinitely, we will serve our God *forever*—in these latter years of the Church Age, in the thousand-year reign of Christ, and in the eternal kingdom of God: "And his servants shall serve him [forever]" (Rev. 22:3). The ways we serve Him are many. Our spiritual gifts and callings make us very useful presently as counselors, exhorters, administrators, donors, helpers, witnesses, evangelists, prophets, teachers, and pastors. In times to come we will help the Potter's Son rule the whole earth, if we willingly suffer for Him in this world. Furthermore, a mature man or woman of God is a rare and beautiful sight in this sinful world. When its inhabitants see the unique beauty of the Potter's glaze in our lives—"this mystery among the Gentiles, which is *Christ in you, the hope of glory*" (Col. 1:27)—they are arrested and compelled to consider the claims of Christ. And as they do so, they are drawn to the heavenly Potter's house, the church; to His Son, the Savior; and to the Potter, in whose presence is the fullness of joy. By doing our part as vessels of honor, we fulfill this, our destiny to honor our Creator.

Indeed, there is something about *clay* that speaks of you and me and every offspring of Adam. The Bible reveals that we were originally made of earth, "And the Lord God formed man of the dust of the ground" (Gen. 2:7), and that when our bodies expire, they will return to dust, "… till thou return unto the ground; for out of it was thou taken: for dust thou art, and unto dust shalt thou return" (Gen. 3:19). So it is entirely natural that the Lord should use the process of making earthen pottery to teach us how He conforms us to His Son's image.

David considered himself to be clay in God's hands: "Thy hands have made me and fashioned me" (Ps. 119:73). Isaiah affirmed this view: "We are the clay, and thou our potter" (Isa. 64:8). The apostle Paul reaffirmed it: "We are his workmanship, [re]created in Christ Jesus unto good works, which God hath before ordained that we should walk in them" (Eph. 2:10). He also compared Christians to clay vessels containing the priceless treasure of Jesus: "We have this treasure in earthen vessels" (2 Cor. 4:7). And Jeremiah gave us God's definitive word on the subject when he instructed Baruch to write, "Behold, as the clay is in the potter's hand, so are ye in mine hand" (Jer. 18:6).

This chapter's biblical analogy explains the purpose for which many people and trials have entered our lives since we have received Christ. Their presence is not accidental. The heavenly Potter has sent them! "This thing is from me" (1 Kings 12:24). They are either instruments in His hands—a rib, trimming tool, or piece of sandpaper. Or they are some part of the Potter's house—His wheel, drying shelf, or fiery kiln. But whatever their specific assignments, the Potter has sent them to transform us into "vessel(s) unto honor, sanctified, and fit for the master's use, and prepared unto every good work" (2 Tim. 2:21). It is absolutely vital that we see *Him* in every circumstance of our lives and cooperate, not contend, with the current phase of our development. "It is the LORD; let him do what seemeth to him good" (1 Sam. 3:18).

If we allow ourselves to be formed by the heavenly Potter, we are on our way to becoming one of His choice vessels—with wings.

Chapter Two

THE WAYS OF EAGLE CHRISTIANS

There are . . . things which are too wonderful for
me . . . the way of an eagle in the air . . .
—PROVERBS 30:18–19

I NSPIRED BY GOD'S wonders in nature, King Agur
declared that, wise as he was, there were still some
things he could not fully grasp. One of these mysteries was, in his own words, "the way of an eagle in the air"
(Prov. 30:19). That is, he wondered how such a large bird
like the eagle so smoothly and easily operates—mounting up, gliding, flying, and diving—in the realm of thin

air. Indeed this spectacle in the sky has captivated many naturalists down through the centuries. But why is Agur's wonder cited in the Bible?

We may surmise several probable reasons. It may be God's way of stimulating Christians' curiosity about nature. Perhaps the Creator wants us to better appreciate His rich and fabulously diverse creation. Or the eagle may be mentioned here to stimulate naturalists' curiosity about God. Perhaps as they ponder the intelligent design and instinctive behavior of the creature the Spirit will draw them to saving faith in the invisible Creator. Whether or not these things are so, I have come to one firm conclusion: this reference to the eagle holds significant figurative meaning for thoughtful Christians. "The way of an eagle in the air" speaks of the eagle Christian, or overcomer, flying high, majestically, gracefully, and victoriously through life, passing with divine ease through this deadly devilish world ruled by the hostile "prince of the power of the air" (Eph. 2:2). To fully grasp the Bible's figurative message, we must understand the natural phenomena involved. So let's examine the eagle more closely.

While there are approximately sixty species of eagles in the world, we will focus on the characteristics of two, the golden eagle and the bald eagle.[1] The biblical eagle may very well be the golden eagle, because its geographic range is Palearctic (all of the Eurasian land mass, the Arabian peninsula, and North Africa), which includes Palestine. But the golden eagle's habitat is also Nearctic (found throughout North America), and it shares many, though not all, physical and behavioral traits with the

North American bald eagle, with which we are more familiar. Therefore, we will use the characteristics of both in describing the ways of eagle Christians.

THE WAYS OF EAGLE CHRISTIANS

"The way of an eagle in the air" refers directly to the following truths about eagles and, indirectly, to those describing their spiritual counterparts, eagle Christians.

Mounting up

In both well-known and obscure references, the Bible describes eagles "mounting up": "They that wait upon the LORD shall . . . *mount up with wings like eagles*" (Isa. 40:31). "Doth the eagle *mount up* at thy command . . .?" (Job 39:27). What does this mean?

When traveling across the land, and especially during migrations, eagles prefer to ride "thermals" (rising currents of warm air) or other updrafts (winds hitting obstructions, such as cliffs, and being redirected upwards). Rather than flap their wings rapidly as smaller birds do, eagles gracefully take to the air with a few slow, powerful strokes of their wings and search for the nearest thermal or updraft. Once inside it, they simply stretch out their substantial wings (spanning six to seven feet) and, holding them virtually still, circle higher and higher on the up-rushing air currents. After reaching a sufficiently high altitude, they glide downward in the direction they are traveling until they find another thermal or updraft; then they repeat the process. Therefore, in their migratory flights, eagles depend not on their own limited strength but on the unlimited power of the wind currents on which they glide. Theirs is an easy way to fly, maximizing gliding and minimizing wing action. This describes the phenomenon of "how an eagle glides through the sky" (Prov. 30:19, TLB).

Our life in Christ can be just as easy. Jesus declared, "My yoke is easy, and my burden is light" (Matt. 11:30). Our daily walk with God is easy or hard depending chiefly on whether we are learning to catch the warm "updrafts" of the Holy Spirit that are available to us. What are these winds of the Spirit? They are all the various means by which we are refilled with the Spirit, edified in our faith, and restored in strength. Some common spiritual thermals available to every Christian are public worship and praise, Bible studies, prayer meetings, Christian conferences and seminars, and meaningful fellowship with serious Christians. But there is more.

The most powerful updraft we can catch is our private time with God. As we worship, pray, and feed on God's Word in our private chambers, especially early in the morning as we begin our day, we enter into the powerful flow of the Spirit that takes us up, up, up—and we slowly and quietly rise into the higher viewpoint of the mind of Christ; the higher graces of the love, patience, and forbearance of God; the higher purposes of God's will, especially His plan for the church; the higher strength of God Himself; and the highest faith, unshakable confidence that knows "God is faithful" (1 Cor. 10:13), always. Such updrafts completely restore our souls when we are exhausted or discouraged.

They refit us for our daily walk and work. Isaiah declared, "They that wait upon the LORD shall renew their strength; [and as they do so] they shall mount up with wings as eagles; [and as they continue doing so] they shall run, and not be weary; and they shall walk, and not faint [thus flowing in the steady, inexhaustible strength of God or the omnipotent 'wind' of His Spirit]" (Isa. 40:31).

These powerful, uplifting Spirit-flows are the secret to easy living in Jesus. They enable us to soar above carnal attitudes, disruptive emotions, and foolish choices that irritate, intimidate, or frustrate us, leaving us confused and exhausted by day's end.

Have you caught a Holy Spirit–thermal today? Or are you depending on your own "wing-strength" to keep you aloft?

Steady in flight

Eagles are very steady in flight. Because of their larger size and weight (eight to thirteen pounds, thirty to thirty-five inches from beak to tail), they are not easily blown off course by high winds as smaller birds may be. Edwin Way Teale wrote:

> Above all other birds it is the soaring eagle, with its size and weight, that gives the most abiding impression of power and purpose in the air. It advances solidly like a great ship cleaving the swells and thrusting aside the smaller waves. It sails directly, where lesser birds are rocked and tilted by the air currents.[2]

Stirred by the "prince of the power of the air," the winds of trouble inevitably come against believers to blow us off our presently productive courses of spiritual growth or effective ministry. We must determine not to be moved by this satanically inspired (though divinely planned and permitted) turbulence. The apostle Paul "flew" steadily through many spiritual storms. When buffeted by the news that serious trouble awaited him in Jerusalem he declared, "None of these things move me" (Acts 20:24), and kept flying straight and steady toward God's goal. When gusts of doubt and unbelief later knocked his fellow believers into a downward spiral of despair, Paul set his face and flew through a vicious Mediterranean hurricane and the fear it spawned, confessing boldly, "I believe God, that it shall be even as it was told me" (Acts 27:25). The weight of his faith and size of his heart made him very stable in these perilous spiritual "flights."

Are we becoming steady and unmovable in our "flight" through this troublesome world? Do we have in us enough weight of the Word, fullness of the Spirit, and courage of heart to be rendered immovable? "Be ye steadfast, unmovable, always abounding in the work of the Lord, forasmuch as ye know that your labor is not in vain in the Lord" (1 Cor. 15:58).

Flying high, seeing far

Eagles can fly very high. While most species of birds fly under five hundred feet (under three thousand during migration), eagles are among the comparatively few birds that fly much higher. Bald eagles have been sighted at altitudes as high as ten thousand feet and golden eagles as high as eleven thousand feet. Some exceptional eagles fly even higher. The U.S. Geological Survey states that an eagle carcass was found in the Himalayas at an altitude of twenty-six thousand feet![3] At such high altitudes eagles obviously have much less chance of colliding with terrain obstructions, such as mountains, cliffs, trees, towers, and buildings, as other birds do. They are also much closer to the sun. Because of their reputation as high fliers, eagles have been described poetically by Christian authors as birds that fly away to look into the sun and touch the face of God. From these heights, theirs is an exceptionally heavenly perspective of this world and its activities.

Eagles are also blessed with exceptional distance vision, arguably the best in the entire animal kingdom. Estimates vary, but it is safe to say that eagles have distance vision at least twice, and perhaps as much as four times, as sharp as human beings. With "eagle vision," these magnificent flying hunters can spot rabbits and other prey from distances in excess of one mile. The Book of Job notes, "Upon the crag of the rock . . . from thence she [the eagle] seeketh the prey, and *her eyes behold afar off*" (Job 39:28–29).

Similarly, "eagle" Christians learn to fly high and develop remarkable distance vision. As eagles take the long view of the countryside, so eagle Christians take the long view of life, living not for today but for eternity, loving not the passing things of the world but the enduring things of God (1 John 2:15–17). Studying and believing Bible prophecy enables them to rise and soar above the turbulent and entangling squabbles of current events and to focus on preparing themselves and others for the approaching epochal appearing of Jesus. Prayerful meditation on God's Word further enables them to be spiritually minded when confronting people and circumstances and thus less inclined to engage in fruitless, low-level contentions over selfish ends. It also gives them invaluable spiritual insight.

Eagle Christians see spiritually beneficial meanings, messages, and revelations in Bible passages that others do not see. Furthermore, God gives them understanding of their times. The all-knowing Holy Spirit enables them to see the spiritual significance or folly of what is going on in their generation. Hence they become like the sons of Issachar, who "had understanding of the times, to know what Israel [God's people] ought to do" (1 Chron. 12:32). Their spiritual vision is further sharpened by trusting and obeying God in numerous trials, so much so that they eventually discern good from evil at considerable distances—who is friend and foe, sincere and insincere, God's servant and Satan's; what is God's plan and what is Satan's diversion; what is sound doctrine and what is heresy. Thus, by flying high and seeing far, they share God's perspective of life in this world.

Consequently, instead of getting bogged down in political power struggles, media frenzies, religious fads, and trivial pursuits that distract many, they soar to new heights daily, drawing near the Son, and lovingly touching and caressing the face of God, their heavenly Father.

You were made to fly high and see far in Christ. Are you doing so?

Nesting high

Eagles nest high, defend their nests, and continue building them yearly. Golden eagles nest high on rock cliffs, sometimes as high as three hundred feet off the ground: "Doth the eagle . . . *make her nest on high*? She dwelleth and abideth on the [high] rock, upon the crag of the [high] rock" (Job 39:27–28). Bald eagles prefer to build their nests, or aeries (pronounced *AIR-eez*), in or near the top of large trees near rivers or lakes. Strongly territorial, eagles will vigorously defend their nesting areas against intruding animals, fowls, or, in rare cases, humans. And they build their nests continuously, each year adding more sticks to the pile and fresh grasses and leaves to the bed atop it for comfort. Unlike most bird nests, eagles' roosts are not bowl-shaped but are instead flat on top; over time they may grow to be as much as twenty feet deep.

Like their counterparts in the bird kingdom, eagle Christians prefer to nest in high places—in the very presence of God. They build their nests, or places of spiritual refuge, rest, and restoration, chiefly by meditating on the highest thoughts comprehendible to the human mind, the lofty logos, the inspired Word of the immortal God: "In his law [Word] doth he mediate day and night" (Ps. 1:2). (See Isaiah 55:8–9.) And they add fresh materials—more of the Spirit's comforting fullness—to their nests daily by praying, giving thanks, sitting silently in God's presence, and worshiping and singing to Him. Jesus had this "nest building" in mind when He said, "If you abide [nest] in me [daily], and my words abide in you [daily] . . ." (John 15:7).

In this way, eagle Christians build an elevated, private, spiritual nesting place, or "secret place" (Ps. 91:1), in which, like eagles, they feed, rest, find warmth, and take refuge from the cruel enemies and recurring storms of life. And they wisely continue building them all their lives by incorporating any means of preparation, practice, or habit that enhances their "nest time" with God. They also diligently defend their nests. When troublemakers and trials try to hinder or spoil their vital communion with God, they do *whatever it takes* to maintain their close, personal fellowship with Jesus. This involves practicing Christian virtues like forgiving, seeking forgiveness, doing good, speaking out, reconciling, separating, giving, receiving, to give a few examples. Thus by nesting high, they are prepared to fly high daily.

Are you nesting high? Or are you seeking refuge, rest, and restoration at lower elevations, trying to draw strength and inspiration from the weak and uninspired things of this present world?

Flying swiftly

Eagles fly very swiftly, especially when they attack their prey. A golden eagle can fly approximately thirty to thirty-five miles per hour in level flight (even faster when chasing prey) and eighty to one hundred (to one hundred fifty, by some estimates) miles per hour in a dive.[4] In numerous references the Bible attests to the eagles' swiftness in flight: "a nation . . . *as swift as the eagle flieth*" (Deut. 28:49). "They [King Saul and Jonathan] were *swifter than eagles*" (2 Sam. 1:23). Nebuchadnezzar's horses were *"swifter than eagles*" (Jer. 4:13). Swift flight is just one of the innate gifts God has given to the eagle.

The eagle is a *raptor,* which is a Latin word for "one who seizes by force." The eagle is specially made to seek, seize, and devour prey. In addition to its exceptional size, speed, and eyesight, it is equipped with a large, hooked beak, and two large feet, each having four very strong toes capped with sharp, hooked "talons." When the eagle seeks and seizes its prey, it is merely fulfilling the purpose for which it was created—it is *doing God's will.* A golden eagle can carry away prey weighing almost as much as it does (eight pounds), but it usually seizes smaller animals. Golden eagles prefer rabbits or hares, while bald eagles seek fish. (Both will eat carrion if other food is not available.) Flying low over the countryside or water, eagles first spot their prey and then suddenly dive and seize it without warning, usually killing their victims immediately with their sharp talons.[5] Noting the eagle's speed in hunting, the Book of Job states, "As the eagle that *hasteneth to the prey*" (Job 9:26).

Just as eagles are swift in flight and even swifter in hunting prey for survival, so eagle Christians are quick to do God's will. They quickly recognize God's plans, as Abraham did when he realized that the ram caught in a thicket was the sacrifice God had provided as a substitute for Isaac. They are swift to follow God's guidance, as the apostle Paul did, who, after receiving a vision calling him to go to Macedonia, "immediately" sailed for that region (Acts 16:10). They are quick to speak for God, as Philip did, who promptly approached and preached Christ to the Ethiopian eunuch after the Spirit told him to "go near" (Acts 8:29). They are quick to give to needy Christians, as the Antioch Christians did, who promptly sent an offering to the notoriously poor Judean saints after the prophet Agabus revealed that a great famine was coming (Acts 11:27–30). As "the eagle that hasteneth to eat" (Hab. 1:8), they are quick to feed on the spiritual food God provides, as the Berean Christians did, who swiftly confirmed Paul's teachings with personal Bible studies of their own.

Eagle Christians are also quick to receive instruction, as Apollos did, who promptly received the vital doctrinal revelations offered him by Paul's companions in ministry, Aquila and Priscilla (Acts 18:24–26). They are quick to correct themselves when they realize that their words, actions, or courses are contrary to God's Word or will, as Paul did, who made a sudden about-face when he realized that he had disobeyed Scripture by speaking disrespectfully to the high priest (Acts 23:1–5)! They are quick to contend for the faith, as Paul and Barnabas did, who, when they encountered false teachings in Antioch, immediately appealed to the apostolic leadership of the Jerusalem church for a definitive ruling (Acts 15:1–2). And they are swift to forgive penitent offenders, as Joseph did, who tearfully received and comforted his brothers the moment he saw that, indeed, they were changed men (Gen. 45:1–8).

Are we "swift as eagles" to do God's will once we know it and have opportunity to discharge it? Or are we slow as crows, sitting around on telephone lines wasting precious time in idle chatter and inexcusable inaction?

Living faithfully

Monogamous, eagles mate after four years and keep the same mate for life. If their mate dies, however, they will take another. Hence, they're faithful, not faithless, true, not treacherous, to their mate and their nest.

Similarly, eagle Christians who marry maintain their fidelity to their spouse. Heeding the clarion call of Christ, the Chief Eagle, they determine to live as He instructed us: "What, therefore, God hath joined together, let not man put asunder" (Matt. 19:6), and as His special apostle, Paul, enjoined: "Let not the wife depart from her husband . . . and let not the husband put away his wife" (1 Cor. 7:10–11). Only in the exceptional cases of death, abandonment, or impenitent adultery will eagle Christians terminate their sacred, lifelong marriage bonds.

They are also very careful to respect other couples' unions, never flirting with or romantically involving themselves with those who are bound in holy wedlock. Why? Because they fear "the Lord," who "is the avenger of all such [who are wronged by adultery]" (1 Thess. 4:6). Also, they understand that Jesus is looking for faithful, not faithless Christians to reside and rule with Him forever. Hence our temporal, earthly marriages are tests given us by which we may qualify for our eternal, heavenly marriage to the Lamb. God knows that if we won't be faithful to our earthly spouses in this world, we won't be faithful to Jesus in the next. But do we know it?

Are we faithful to our spouse in our present marriage? Are we respecting the sanctity of other marriages?

If so, we're proving our readiness to wed the soon-coming Bridegroom and live and labor faithfully with Him.

Heaven bound

Describing how quickly our money seems to depart from us, the Book of Proverbs says that "riches certainly make themselves wings . . . [and] they *fly away like an eagle toward heaven*" (Prov. 23:5). This verse alludes to the way eagles spread their great wings and, leaving the limitations, strife, and confusion of this world behind, gracefully fly away into the heavens. Hence, they are not earth-bound but heaven-bound creatures.

Similarly, the overcoming Christian is a heaven-bound creature. He learns to spread his spiritual wings and, leaving all earthly trials and troublemakers behind, fly away to the presence of God. How? He does so in at least four distinct ways.

First, we fly heavenward when we abandon temporal, worldly goals and fix our hearts on eternal, heavenly ends: "If ye, then, be risen with Christ, seek those things which are above. . . . *Set your affection on things above*, not on things on the earth" (Col. 3:1–2). Until we make this first "flight," we will be unable to make the others. Second, we spread our heart wings and fly off into blissful communion with Jesus every day by private prayer, prayerful Bible study, and the reading of devotional and other edifying materials. Thus, we answer Jesus' vital calling not only to *believe* on Him, but also to "*be* with him" (Mark 3:14). Third, we fly away to heaven by entering fully and freely into the expression of our local church's praise and worship. "As they ministered to the Lord" (Acts 13:2), the leaders of the church at Antioch "flew" so close to God they could hear His still, small voice, saying, "Separate me Barnabas and Saul for the work unto which I have called them" (v. 2). Delightful in normal times, such "heavenly flights" are vital releases, or internal deliverances, that sustain us through severe times. For instance, as Paul and Silas prayed and sang praises in the inner prison at Philippi, God suddenly opened every door and released them from their unjust and cruel affliction. Fourth, our final "flight" will occur at the end of this life.

For many Christians, this will happen the moment their bodies expire. Then, in a moment, their spirits will leave their bodies and they will fly away into the immediate presence of God: "to be absent from the body . . . [is] to be [immediately] present with the Lord" (2 Cor. 5:8). But for many other overcoming Christians living in these "last days," the Rapture of the church will be our terminal heavenly ascent. When God blows His trumpet and Jesus suddenly appears in the heavens, eagle Christians all over the earth will spread their wings and, in the twinkling of an eye, rise to meet Him in the air: "Then we who are alive and remain shall be *caught up together with them in the clouds to meet the Lord in the air*; and so shall we ever be with him" (1 Thess. 4:17). (See also 1 Corinthians 15:51–53; Colossians 3:4.) It will be the greatest spiritual thermal we ever ride and the greatest gathering of eagle Christians in the church's long history.

Are you learning to spread your soul wings and fly away into the presence of God now? In the desires of your heart? In your private communion? In your public expression of praise and worship? Are you preparing for your "last flight," either at your bodily expiration or at Jesus' bodily appearing? If so, you're a true eagle Christian—heaven bound!

Renewing their strength

An eagle's energy is depleted daily by lengthy flights, hunts, vigorous chases, and struggles to obtain food from other eagles or predators when prey is scarce. To survive, therefore, an eagle must renew its strength. It does this primarily by feeding and rest. As it feasts on live prey or carrion, or rests in its aerie far above its predators, the eagle's strength is restored.

Like eagles, our strength is restored primarily by feeding and rest. When our souls are spiritually drained by life, labor, or ministry, we restore our spiritual energy by feeding on God's Word. The psalmist declares this to be one of the most precious benefits of our salvation: "Bless the LORD, O my soul . . . who satisfieth thy mouth with good things [literal and spiritual food], so that thy youth is renewed like the eagle's (Ps. 103:1, 5). When weakened by anxiety, doubt, discouragement, or failure, our souls can be replenished by simply choosing to put our trust again in the faithful character and promises of God: "O God . . . in thee do I put my trust" (Ps. 16:1). To believe God fully without reservation brings us rest from the agitation of fear—"We who have *believed* do enter into *rest*" (Heb. 4:3)—and a fresh refilling of rejuvenating life from God. As we do these things, the Chief Eagle restores our spiritual strength: "He restoreth my soul" (Ps. 23:3). And when we are physically tired or exhausted, we restore our bodily strength by taking proper rest. There are also other means by which we renew our spiritual strength.

For example, the loving exhortations—urgings to faith, righteousness, duty, perseverance, love, and sacrifice—of our fellow eagle Christians renew us, as do also authentic prophetic utterances. Jonathan's timely prophetic exhortation boosted David's trust in God (1 Sam. 23:16–17). The mystical yet real touches of angels also fortify us, as they frequently did Daniel (Dan. 10:18–19). Good news reinvigorates us when we're flagging. Jacob was a tired, old eagle when one day he heard a report that was beyond anything he had ever dreamed: Joseph was alive, governor of mighty Egypt, and inviting his dad to a reunion! And suddenly, "The spirit of Jacob . . . revived" (Gen. 45:27). Fulfillment of God's long-delayed plans rejuvenates us: "Hope deferred maketh the heart sick, but when the desire cometh, it is a tree [source] of life" (Prov. 13:12); or, "It is new life to have desire fulfilled" (Moffatt). Prayer, especially in the spirit, is a tremendous spiritual edifier: "But ye, beloved, building up yourselves on your most holy faith, praying in the Holy Spirit" (Jude 20). Surely this is why Paul urged the Ephesians, and us, to practice "Praying always with all prayer and supplication in the Spirit" (Eph. 6:18). Answers to prayer, especially urgently needed ones, restore our youthful joy: "Ask, and ye shall receive, that your joy may be full" (John 16:24). Visits from loving friends bolster us when we're sick, imprisoned, troubled, or persecuted. Of his frequent visitor Onesiphorus, the imprisoned apostle Paul wrote, "He often refreshed me" (2 Tim. 1:16). And special messages, dreams, and visions from God also refill eagle Christians with the iron of life. When troubled in Corinth by the prospect of yet another attack from his persecutors, Paul received a vision in the night in which Jesus reassured him he would not be assaulted or injured again in that city and was therefore to "speak, and hold not thy peace" (Acts 18:9). Strengthened, Paul, whom I consider the church's bravest war eagle, continued fighting the good fight in Corinth for eighteen more months (v. 11).

Are you a worn and weary eagle Christian? If so, don't fold your wings and faint. Instead, by the means described above, prayerfully seek and receive the renewing of your soul and body. You have a lot of soaring in the Spirit and hastening after God's will yet to do. Also, many eaglet Christians need your help.

Eaglets have it easy

For about ten to thirteen weeks after hatching, eaglets remain in their parents' nests. They grow rapidly, becoming nearly one foot tall at three weeks and almost as large as their parents at six. During this time their life is, well, easy! Their days are spent waiting for their parents to bring them food, during which watches they alternately sleep, eat, stretch their wings, clumsily hop around their increasingly crowded nests, or play with the "toys" their parents bring, such as rocks, man-made objects (shoes, gloves, light bulbs), or other attention grabbers randomly discovered. At night, they are brooded, or sheltered and warmed by their parents' wings and bodies. Since they can't fly yet, eaglets don't hunt. This is done for them by their attentive, loving parents.

What a fitting parallel this is to the life of a newly born-again Christian. After conversion, the believer is a spiritual eaglet in the "nest" of the local church or fellowship, and life is easier then than at any other time. His (or her) free time is taken up largely with easy, pleasant, faith-related activities: feeding on Bible readings, teachings, and sermons; sharing fellowship meals and Communion tables; waiting on the next prayer or worship service; and perhaps attempting, however clumsily, to tell others what Jesus has done for him or explain newly discovered Bible truths.

The eaglet Christian enjoys being brooded over, sheltered and warmed by the wise counsel, timely exhortations, and loving fellowship of more experienced Christians. He also begins experiencing the wondrous brooding of God, the unmatched comfort that comes when the Lord Himself spreads His wings over, or manifests His presence to, His developing spiritual eagle. This gives him reassurance, confirmation, and strength: "He shall cover thee with his feathers, and under his wings shalt thou trust" (Ps. 91:4). Some eaglet Christians also get very excited about the curious "toys" they find in their Bible studies and church meetings. For example, they become elated over the gifts, operations, and utterances of the Spirit; the *dunamis* power of God in healing and delivering the oppressed; and the sheer excitement of rejoicing and praising God with many others of like faith. And they love the many activities of the church, including its charities, missions, meetings, plans, and programs.

(I use "toys" here, not to signify worthlessness or irrelevance, but rather to describe *objects of excessive interest,* though they are biblically based, wholly of God, and vital in their proper time and place.) Indeed their Spirit-filled "nest" has much to investigate, taste, digest, and enjoy.

During this time God, acting as a heavenly parent Eagle, deliberately holds off the pressures that young believers cannot yet bear, such as strong tests of bitter persecution, puzzling protracted trials of faith, stunning crosses of injustice or betrayal, and the rigorous labors of fivefold ministry. Later these spiritual eaglets will "fly off" by faith into the elevated lifestyle marked by consistent biblical thinking, spiritual living, and divine guidance, where they will assume the higher duties of effective church work, Christian ministry, and missions. For now, however, God's plan is for others to discharge these responsibilities for them—feeding them fresh meat from the Word, praying down upon them the living water and blessings of the Spirit, going out on evangelistic "hunts" to call the lost to salvation, leading the church, and dealing with its many problems—while He broods over His eaglets.

Luke described the first "nest" in which Christian eaglets took refuge in Jerusalem: "And they continued steadfastly in the apostles' doctrine and fellowship, and in breaking of bread, and in prayers . . . praising God, and having favor with all the people" (Acts 2:42, 47). During this initial time in the "nest," the first Christians had it easy. And so do eaglet Christians today.

But the easiness of spiritual infancy eventually gives way to the healthy challenges of spiritual growth.

Teaching their young to fly

Moses described in detail how eagles teach their young to fly: "As an eagle stirreth up her nest, fluttereth over her young, spreadeth abroad her wings, taketh them [her eaglets], beareth them on her wings . . ." (Deut. 32:11). Then he revealed that God trains His people in a similar way to live by faith in Him: ". . . So the LORD alone did lead him [Israel]" (v. 12).

In nature this process of training eaglets to fly unfolds as follows. When the eaglets are ten to thirteen weeks old, the adult eagles begin to disturb the nest, removing the grasses and leaves that have made it comfortable during the brooding stage: "As an eagle stirreth up her nest . . ." It is an inaudible but clear announcement that change is imminent, that brooding time is over and the time to fly is at hand. During this period, the parents fly off to hunt and purposely return with increasingly less food for the eaglets. Consequently, the eaglets begin to grow very hungry.[6]

At times the parents spread their substantial wings while standing in the nest to demonstrate to the eaglets the superb flying equipment they have at their disposal: "As an eagle . . . spreadeth abroad her wings." For inspiration, they hover on updrafts near the nest, again showing their young how easy it is to mount up, glide, and fly: "As an eagle . . . fluttereth over her young." And to benevolently provoke them, they sometimes do this with choice pieces of food dangling from their talons—fish, rabbits, or rodents—yet without giving them to the eaglets. Eventually this tough love and sign language gets the message through: "If you want to eat, you have to fly and hunt just as we do!" So, moved beyond themselves by their parents' training and their stomachs' aching, the young eaglets make their first flight, usually gliding directly to earth with a somewhat tumbling, out-of-control landing due to their lack of experience in using their wings and tail feathers to slow their landing speed. Afterwards, through practice, they gradually perfect the various skills of take off, flight, and landing.

The last phrase of this text, "As an eagle . . . taketh them [her young], [and] beareth them on her wings," implies two other remote possibilities. First, if eaglets are stubbornly reluctant to take their first flight, their parents graciously force them to do so, perhaps by using their powerful talons to grasp their eaglets' bodies and their substantial wing-power to lift them out of the nest and drop them. Thanks, Mom and Dad! Second, it suggests the possibility that, if, after such involuntary or voluntary "launching," the eaglets are clearly struggling in their first flight, the parents may intervene, diving toward the frightened eaglets, and grasping them with their powerful feet (much as they do other birds when preying upon them) and in some way guide them to safety or break their fall. While no observations of such behavior have been documented by naturalists or ornithologists, those I spoke with agreed that, even if it seems improbable, it is not impossible. Whatever the case, the inspired, inerrant Word of God declares that there was a time when Moses personally observed parent eagles using their powerful wings to in some way "bear," or *carry*, their eaglets while teaching them to fly. So I accept this fact by faith, despite the absence of corroborative scientific evidence or a singular definitive interpretation.

In the same way, God acts toward us as a heavenly Eagle, training us to "fly"; that is, to be spiritually minded and to live by faith in God's faithfulness, follow His guidance, walk in His ways (life disciplines), minister in His ways (methods), and overcome (fly over, glide through) the stressful and dangerous trials we encounter in life. But do we see His hand when He disrupts our comfortable nests and, by His arrangement of circumstances, thrusts us out into new places of living, working, or ministry? Frankly, most of us don't discern His hand working in our strange providences until long after the fact.

For example, God used the rude and violent rejection of the members of Jesus' home synagogue to disrupt His nest in Nazareth and send Him off to Capernaum. (See Luke 4:28–31.) Do we recognize His purpose when He calls us to "hunt," or seek spiritual food, for ourselves in prayerful study of the Bible and no longer depend solely on our pastor to provide our souls' nourishment? Paul charged his protégé Timothy, "[You] Study to show yourself approved unto God . . ." (2 Tim. 2:15).

Or have we discovered yet how wonderful our wings of prayer and praise are and that by using them we can rise and soar above even the most disrupting and damaging stresses of life? Are we willing, when necessary, to leap out of our familiar nests and fly by faith to the next place of living or service God has prepared for us, trusting Jesus to guide us by His Word, voice, presence, and peace, and by the counselors He has given us? Have we realized that during such times we are being carried on wings of intercession, that Jesus is at the Father's right hand, where "he ever liveth to make intercession for us" (Heb. 7:25)? Do we understand that our faithful pastors, elders, mentors, and fellow believers are beating their prayer wings daily so that we may learn to stay aloft? Epaphras' intercessions helped carry the fledgling Colossian Christians: "Epaphras, who is . . . always laboring fervently for you in prayers . . ." (Col. 4:12). Are we willing to humbly cooperate with all these aspects of our "flight training"?

It is important that we heartily answer, "Yes!" Why? Because, simply put, eaglets *must* learn to fly. If they don't fly, they die.

Many eaglets don't survive

Sadly, many eaglets don't survive long. According to one source, as high as 40 percent die during or just after their precarious first flights because they are severely or lethally injured in collisions with rocks or tree limbs.[7] And of those who survive their first flight, many are killed in their first year by a host of besetting perils.

Despite having thousands of insulating feathers (seven thousand for bald eagles), some are killed by prolonged exposure to extremely cold temperatures. Some are shot by hunters, including ranchers who fear golden eagles will kill their young lambs. Some die from contaminated water or the toxins present in their prey; DDT alone killed many eagles in North America in the 1950s and 1960s. One of the most prevalent causes of eaglet deaths are "Cain and Abel struggles," in which the older, larger nestling kills the younger, or deprives it of food to ensure its own nourishment and survival in the nest. Strangely, the eagle parents generally do not interfere with these sibling wars. Some young eagles are killed while fighting with other eagles over prey in areas or conditions where food is scarce. Others die simply because they are poor hunters. And still others perish in senseless accidents caused by such things as contacting power lines or colliding with airplanes (or being ingested by jet engines). Some die from drowning, which occurs when an eagle becomes submerged and his feathers saturated with water while hunting fish. This water-logged condition renders him temporarily unable to fly. If he's too far out to swim back to land (by awkwardly paddling his wings), he'll eventually succumb. Overcoming eaglets, those who survive these dangers, live approximately fifteen to twenty years in the wild. Some live thirty years or more.[8]

Like their counterparts, eagle Christians must learn to overcome a host of dangers tailor-made to prevent them from growing up spiritually and learning to "fly" through life by faith in and obedience to Christ. What are the perils that cut short our spiritual destiny?

Many who are young in the faith are simply disinterested in the things of God. Isaiah wrote with a sigh, "My people doth not consider" (Isa. 1:3). Because they rarely read, and even more rarely study, God's Word, these sickly eaglets never rise and soar in life. Hence, when forced from their protected nests, they fall, offended and disillusioned with the Lord, to the death of their faith. Many others are fatally distracted by the alluring things of the world; they are sucked in by the powerful engines of money-madness or immorality, drowned in materialism, or injured in the struggles of political or ecclesiastical power-seeking. Many die from prolonged exposure to very cold churches, in which the warm fervor of faith, love, and holiness was long ago extinguished. Others give up the faith because of "Cain and Abel struggles," in which sin-hardened Christians reject and persecute them because they envy their faith, gifts, successes, or blessings. Many fail because they're poisoned by deadly attitude toxins, such as unforgiveness, hatred, resentment, murmuring, or pride. These attitudes render them unteachable, stubbornly unwilling to learn from wiser, more experienced pastors, teachers, and elders. For these and other reasons, many Christian converts never rise and fly as full-fledged, spiritually minded disciples and servants of Jesus.

Are any of these threatening conditions taking you down? Or are you learning to consistently discern and avoid them and keep flying?

Eagles don't flock

While most birds are gregarious, eagles generally do not flock. Young eagles who have not yet mated sometimes cluster, but adults usually mate and live in pairs. Compared with many birds, then, the eagle lives a separated life. Exceptions occur in both extremely good and bad conditions. When winters are extremely harsh and prey scarce, eagles cluster wherever food may be found, and, conversely, wherever food is abundant, as it is during the seasonal salmon runs in the Pacific Northwest, they also gather to feed.

Like the eagles, overcoming Christians often live comparatively separated lives. There are several reasons for this. First, they don't blindly follow societal patterns or even popular church trends, but rather they earnestly endeavor to practice biblical values and ways of living. Second, they strive to live sanctified, or holy, lives, so they may be fit for God's use. Hence, they choose not to maintain close friendships with impenitent, practicing sinners or hypocritical or backslidden Christians: "If a man . . . purge [separate] himself from these [dishonorable vessels], he shall be a vessel unto honor, sanctified, and fit for the master's use" (2 Tim. 2:21). Third, their stated position on controversial issues, or in some cases their adversaries' malicious lies, cause others to withdraw from them. Jesus described this when He said, "Blessed are ye, when men shall hate you, and . . . separate you from their company, and shall reproach you . . . for the Son of man's sake" (Luke 6:22). Fourth, as eagles are instinctively called to live faithfully in pairs, God often calls eagle Christians to follow and serve Him "two by two," even as Jesus summoned and sent His original disciples (Mark 1:16–20; 6:7). For these reasons, and especially in times of prevailing lukewarmness or apostasy, eagle Christians are often found in small, very committed churches or among the faithful remnant in larger, less committed churches. In certain nations and cultures, their separation is even more extreme: "Where two or three are gathered together in my name" (Matt. 18:20).

But there are two notable exceptions to the separated lifestyle of eagle Christians: seasons of persecution and revival.

Whenever eagle Christians are rejected or harassed for their faith, obedience, witness, growth, or outreach, other spiritual eagles cluster to help them bear their cross by various means, such as intercession in the Spirit, exhortive communication, financial support, or, in rare cases, circumstantial intervention. Thus they help their own kind in the worst of times.

Conversely, in the best of times, when God pours out His Holy Spirit afresh on His thirsty people, eagle Christians also migrate to these visitations, figuratively (sympathetically, doctrinally, or through media) if not physically. The older, more anointed eagles come to help minister the nourishing Word and saving power of the Chief Eagle to the spiritual eaglets, developing disciples who themselves come to feed on the truths and insights they impart.

The church has seen many great gatherings of its eagles in the best and worst times of its long and storied history. Eagle Christians gathered repeatedly in the streets, prisons, and amphitheatres of various cities, provinces, and nations during the Roman persecution (A.D. 64–313) to support each other as they suffered the loss of reputation, property, and life. They did it again, centuries later, when the dark inquisitors of the Medieval Roman church mercilessly maligned, robbed, imprisoned, tortured, and executed countless enlightened reformers and Protestants. The eagles also came together during the church's most significant outpourings of the Spirit, such as the Great

Awakenings and the notable revivals of the nineteenth and twentieth centuries.

If, due to long separation for righteousness' sake, you are weary, my fellow Christian eagle, take heart. A great gathering of eagles is coming. When the mighty wind of the Spirit refills the remnant church (the body of true believers among the larger body of professed Christians) in these last days to finish God's work in, among, and through us, eagle Christians worldwide will be drawn together in varying degrees of personal contact and cooperation in ministry. And, thrilled by the most powerful and uplifting thermal we've ever ridden, we will revel in sustained holy joy and unprecedented fellowship: "When the LORD turned again the captivity of Zion [the righteous remnant], we were like them that dream. Then was our mouth filled with laughter, and our tongue with singing" (Ps. 126:1–2).

Carried on eagles' wings

Spanning six to seven feet, eagles' wings are among the largest and most powerful in the bird kingdom. In North America, only condors have a larger wingspan. The aerodynamic shape, large surface, and intelligently designed feather placement of eagles' wings make them perfectly suited for both *maximum lift* and *swift flight*. Hence eagles can quickly and powerfully snatch up, not only vulnerable prey, but also their own small eaglets when threatened, and carry them far away.

God does the same for us, His children. When we are greatly stressed or long oppressed, and about to snap, collapse, or give up, He suddenly and powerfully intervenes to carry us away to safety. Describing His deliverance of the Israelites from Egyptian bondage, God said, "I bore you on eagles' wings and brought you unto myself" (Exod. 19:4).

And He will do the same for Israel in the last days. In Israel's worst hour, the coming "time of Jacob's trouble" (Jer. 30:7), known to us as the tribulation period, God will twice swiftly and powerfully intervene to carry away His faithful remnant of believing Jews to safety.

First, at or near the midpoint of that seven-year time of unprecedented trouble, He will suddenly translate— snatch away from the earth and change from a mortal to an immortal state—the 144,000 Jewish male evangelists and the vast number of Jews and Gentiles saved and taught through their exceptionally empowered and effective ministries. (See Revelation 7:1–8, 9–14, esp. vv. 9, 13–14; 12:5b.) Thus they will experience the *maximum lift* of the divine Eagle's wings. This stunning "second Rapture" will enrage Antichrist and move him to denounce and militarily attack Israel, declare himself God, and demand that the whole world worship him alone. Second, the Lord will then make a way for the remaining converted Jews to swiftly flee, according to Christ's explicit instructions (Matt. 24:15–16), and be hidden and sustained on earth for the remaining three and a half years (Rev. 12:6). John described their divinely assisted flight to safety as a woman being carried on eagles' wings: "And to the woman [the faithful remnant of Israel] were given *two wings of a great eagle*, that she might *fly into the wilderness*, into her place, where she is nourished for a time, and times, and half a time, from the face of the serpent" (Rev. 12:14). So this remnant of Jewish believers in Christ will experience the *swift flight* of God's large and powerful wings of deliverance.

Have we ever realized that we too have a keen-eyed, faithful, all-powerful, divine Eagle watching over us? Do we believe that when we can go no farther He will in some way swoop down to save us? In His unfailing faithfulness, He will always provide either *maximum lift* or *swift flight (escape)*. In the first case, He will superbly and supernaturally uphold, strengthen, and assist us in the midst of the trouble: "Fear thou not; for I am with thee . . . I will *strengthen* thee . . . *help* thee . . . I will *uphold* thee" (Isa. 41:10). In the second, He will swiftly and powerfully release us from our trying circumstances: "God is faithful, who will . . . make the way to *escape*" (1 Cor. 10:13). The last and greatest instance of this in the Church Age will be the Rapture. When God's work in us and our work in this world is finished, we will be suddenly, supernaturally transported to heaven "on eagles' wings."

In your present tribulation, are you afraid that the divine Eagle will callously fly by you or lift you up briefly only to drop you to your death on your rocky problems below? Have you, as the disciples did, resorted to panic prayers? "Master, carest thou not that we perish?" (Mk. 4:38). Or are you expecting to be carried all the way to safety "on eagles' wings"?

Invited to dine at the King's table

Great honors await those who consistently live as eagle Christians. One of those distinctions will be an invitation to dine with the heavenly Father and Son at the marriage supper of the Lamb in heaven. A banquet like no other, it will occur in two stages and involve two vastly different groups of attendees.

The spiritual eagles, or mature Christians, will be the first to dine. As the seven years of the tribulation near their awesome conclusion on earth, all the translated, overcoming Christians in heaven will gather and, by special invitation, sit and sup with the Savior at His joyful wedding banquet: "And he saith unto me, Write, [Supremely] Blessed are they who are called unto the marriage supper of the Lamb" (Rev. 19:9). Contrary to popular teaching and wishful thinking, not every Christian will receive an invitation. Scripture reveals that carnal and apostate Christians, as well as Christ-rejecting Jews, will not be there. (See Matthew 22:1–14.) Throughout history, it has been customary for children to dine first, and then for their pets to eat, usually on the scraps (Matt. 15:26–27). Hence, immediately after God's children feast in heaven, their "pets" will feed on earth. Let me explain.

As the marriage supper ends in heaven, Antichrist's armies will gather on earth to battle Christ at Armageddon. Christ, accompanied with heavenly armies of overcomers and angels, will then return to earth and slay those gathered to defy Him. Immediately afterwards, an angel will summon all the birds (who along with all other creatures in the animal kingdom constitute the "pets" of Adam, who originally named them and enjoyed their company, and his descendants, who do the same) on earth to the battlefield so that they may feed on the unprecedented massive carnage. Macabre as it sounds, this grisly feeding will be their portion of the great marriage supper: "And I saw an angel . . . and he cried with a loud voice . . . to *all the fowls* that fly in the midst of heaven, *Come and gather yourselves together unto the supper of the great God*, that ye may *eat the flesh of kings . . . captains . . . mighty men, and . . . horses*" (Rev. 19:17–18; see v. 21b). Matthew reveals that when Jesus foretold this, He specifically mentioned, and so gave priority to, the presence of eagles: "For wherever the carcass is, there will the *eagles* be gathered together" (Matt. 24:28). Luke agreed, quoting Jesus as saying, "Wherever the body is [bodies or carcasses are], there will the *eagles* be gathered together" (Luke 17:37). The Book of Job also alludes to this: "Her [the eagle's] young ones also suck up blood; and where the slain are, there is she" (Job 39:30). So while all birds will be needed and invited to consume the massive carnage at Armageddon, the eagles will sit first at the final banquet of the birds. The words of King Jesus reveal that He has reserved this honor for them.

Will you be invited to feed at the King's table in heaven? This may depend upon how regularly you feed at His table on earth: "Thou preparest a table [of blessings] before me [now] in the presence of mine enemies" (Ps. 23:5). Are you feeding on the bread of God's Word daily? "Man shall not live by bread alone, but by every word of God" (Luke 4:4). Are you feasting on the messages provided you by your pastors and teachers? Are you receiving and digesting the counsels fed you by your elders, mentors, and counselors? Are you drinking in the truths and insights the King gives you through other anointed ministers? If you feast sumptuously at the King's table now, you will be invited to do the same in heaven. This is just one of the honors the King has reserved for eagle Christians.

Invited to participate in the King's judgment

While to us it may seem an unwelcome, even reprehensible, duty, participation in the execution of royal enemies is a high honor indeed. So states the sacred psalmist:

> Let the saints be joyful . . . let . . . a two-edged sword [be] in their hand, to execute [God's] vengeance upon the [rebellious] nations, and punishments upon the peoples [who defy the King] . . . to execute upon them the judgment written. *This honor have all his [true] saints* . . .
>
> —PSALM 149:5–9

Before Joshua executed the five Canaanite kings whose armies he defeated at Gibeon, he called his captains to put their feet on their necks (Josh. 10:24). Thus he shared with them, and they undertook with him, the honor of executing these evil kings who were driven with a desire to destroy God's children and thwart His will. Joshua's actions foreshadow Christ's actions at the battle of Armageddon on the plain of Megiddo.

At that scene of many ancient decisive battles, Jesus will grant His brave "captains"—eagle Christians—the honor of participating in His righteous and requisite judgment on Antichrist and the ten kings that lead his international military coalition in their vain attempt to preempt Jesus' return and kingdom. Immediately after the marriage supper of the Lamb, eagle Christians will mount white horses and assist Jesus in routing His enemies: "And the armies that were in heaven followed him upon white horses, clothed in fine linen, white and clean" (Rev. 19:14; see v. 19). "The Lamb shall overcome them [the ten kings] . . . and they that are with him are called, and chosen, and faithful [mature, tested, overcoming believers]" (Rev. 17:14). But one question remains to be posed and pondered.

Will you be invited to execute King Jesus' enemies? That will depend upon whether you are fighting for Him now in this time—fighting the good fight of faith; fighting against sin in your own life and in the church; fighting other spiritual conflicts the Lord calls you to fight in His name. If we won't fight for Jesus now, He won't ask us to fight for Him later. Therefore, we must learn to fight for Him acceptably.

That will demand three things of us. First, we must stop fighting the wrong battles, namely, our personal conflicts or any other diversionary and futile religious, social, or political controversies into which the enemy may try to lure us! If we are preoccupied with fighting the wrong battles, we will neither recognize nor address the right ones. Second, we must learn to let God fight our personal battles for us. Jehoshaphat wisely let the Lord fight his battles: "*The battle* [conflict with your enemies for Jehovah's sake] *is not yours, but God's* . . . Ye shall not need to fight in this battle" (2 Chron. 20:15–17). Third, we must learn to enter into only those conflicts God calls us to fight. Just when David was tempted to fight his own cause against Nabal, Abigail wisely reminded him he was called to fight *God's* battles, not his own: "My lord fighteth *the battles of the LORD*" (1 Sam. 25:28). Wisely David withdrew from the fight and reserved his energies only for those battles the Lord called him to fight, namely, against the Philistines and other adversaries of Israel. Because David fought the Lord's battles—and only His—on earth, he will undoubtedly be one of the war eagles the Lord invites to fight His final battle. Are we following David's example?

If we fight the Lord's battles, and no others, we too will return with Jesus to Armageddon. And, however gruesome the scene, it will be a great honor to help the King execute His enemies.

Now you are more fully informed about "the way of an eagle in the air," and, more importantly, the ways of eagle Christians.[9]

So *to the sky with you*, my fellow eagle Christian! Fling away your trust in the wisdom and strength of your flesh; rely henceforth only on the power of wind, the mighty wind of the Spirit! Don't cling to your comfortable nest; mount up and fly over the trying people and problems that have harried and hindered you! Scorn the lower altitudes; fly high, majestically, gracefully, and victoriously through life, your face ever set toward and seeking the Son of righteousness!

And as you do so, keep your savor strong.

Chapter Three

THE SALT OF THE EARTH

Ye are the salt of the earth.

—MATTHEW 5:13

*I*N THE FIRST of two similitudes in His Sermon on the Mount, Jesus made a monumental analogy between His devoted followers and salt. Succinctly, His declaration reads, "Ye are the salt of the earth" (Matt. 5:13). Before we can understand the spiritual implications of Jesus' declaration and the crucial clarifying comments He added in the same verse, we should familiarize ourselves with the natural facts about salt.

THE FACTS ABOUT SALT

A full understanding of salt entails knowing its chemical composition, locations, methods of extraction, historic uses, and modern uses. Let's examine these topics.

Its chemical composition

The substance known commonly as "salt" is also known by its chemical name, *sodium chloride*, and its mineral name, *halite*.[1] Sometimes various amounts of other minerals become mixed with sodium chloride. For instance, only 8 percent of the salt in the waters of the Dead Sea is pure sodium chloride, while 53 percent is magnesium chloride and 37 percent is potassium chloride. So, the salt evaporated from its waters is not pure sodium chloride. (Perhaps it was this example Jesus had in mind in our text when He referred to salt that had "lost its savor.") According to the United States government, acceptable food-grade salt, or table salt, must have a pure sodium chloride content of 97.5 percent or higher.[2]

Its location

Simply stated, salt is *everywhere!* It is in the land. Underground salt deposits are located on every continent. Salt is found in the seven seas. The oceans are so full of brine (salt water) that some scientists estimate that if their waters evaporated, the salt left behind would be enough to cover the continental United States with a layer of salt one and

The Salt of the Earth

one-half miles deep! Salt is found in rivers and lakes. As rivers flow over the land, varying amounts of sodium and chlorine in the soil and rocks dissolve into their waters and flow into lakes where, as the fresh water evaporates, the sodium and chlorine settle in higher concentrations. Two famous briny lakes, the Great Salt Lake (USA) and the Dead, or "Salt," Sea (Israel), have a salt content many times *higher* than ocean water. (The Dead Sea has nine times more salinity!) Salt is in the air. Ocean breezes blow "salt spray" into coastal areas, leaving thin but visible salt deposits on the glass and surfaces of automobiles and oceanfront homes and buildings. If not washed off, this salt will form rust on metal surfaces. And, finally, salt is in our bodies. Approximately 1 percent (exactly 0.9 percent) of our blood and body cells are comprised of salt.

Its methods of extraction

In America today, there are three primary means of extracting salt: evaporation (solar method), mining (room-and-pillar mining), and wells (solution mining). In the solar method, large amounts of salt water are directed through a series of evaporating ponds, and, after all the water evaporates, the remaining piles of salt are harvested. In room-and-pillar mining, large deposits of rock salt deep in the earth are mined just like coal. Shafts are dug and chambers are drilled or blasted with explosives, and, after the rock salt is removed, large underground chambers are created with solid salt pillars separating them. Once the solid rock salt is brought to the surface, it is crushed, graded, packed, and shipped. In solution mining, a well is drilled in an underground salt deposit, and two pipes, a smaller one inside of a larger one, are lowered into the well. Pressurized fresh water is then pumped down the smaller inner pipe into the salt deposit where, after it dissolves large quantities of loose and rock salt, it becomes brine. As the water fills the salt deposit, the brine is forced to the surface through the larger pipe. The water is then evaporated and the pure salt harvested.

Its historic uses

From ancient times, salt has been highly valued and used in a variety of ways. Primarily, salt has been used as seasoning. Job said, "Can that which is unsavory [tasteless] be eaten without salt?" (Job 6:6). Another basic and indispensable use has been as a preservative for meat. Before the comparatively recent advent of refrigeration, fish, beef, and pork were salted to prevent spoilage. Salt, which inhibits the growth of bacteria, was also used as an antiseptic. In antiquity, midwives rubbed salt on newborn babies as a primitive method of protecting them against infection. God alluded to this when He compared Jerusalem's original condition to that of an abandoned infant: "Thou wast not salted at all, nor swaddled at all" (Ezek. 16:4).

Salt was an integral part of ancient covenant making. In the East, covenants were sealed with a banquet, at which salt was used as a seasoning and after which Arabs would typically say, "There is salt between us," signifying agreement, friendship, and peace.[3] And salt was synonymous with hospitality. For a visitor or traveler to "eat salt with" someone was to receive his hospitality.[4] Salt was a key part of the Old Testament system of animal sacrifice. God specifically commanded, "With all thine offerings thou shalt offer salt" (Lev. 2:13), and Jesus later added, "Every sacrifice shall be salted with salt" (Mark 9:49). And there's more to the ancient story of salt.

Salt was at times considered as valuable as precious metals and rare spices. It was commonly traded for gold and silver. Some ancient cultures levied taxes on salt, and at one time the Chinese used salt coins for currency. Roman soldiers were occasionally paid partially or wholly in salt, which they then used to barter for other necessary commodities. So common was this practice that we derive the English word *salary* from the Latin word *salarium*, meaning *salt money*. And the commonly used expression that someone is "not worth their salt" means literally, they're not worth the salary they're being paid.

Moreover, salt was a major impetus for road building. Numerous roads were originally constructed mainly to transport salt, and the salt trade helped establish many large and prosperous cities, such as Genoa and Venice. And the story goes on.

Rarer historic uses of salt were in punishment and war. Mariners who were whipped for insubordination or crimes were sometimes afterwards doused with salt water, which made their already painful wounds hurt worse! O, you cruel Captain Bligh! And when armies conquered cities or nations, if they wished to elongate their defeated foes' miseries, they sometimes scattered salt throughout their fields, thus rendering them unfit for agriculture for the foreseeable future. After defeating the city of Shechem, Abimelech and his men "sowed it with salt" (Judg. 9:45).

Its modern uses

Today, salt is still used as the most common seasoning found in our homes and restaurants. And we still use it to preserve meats—I love salt-cured country ham! Additionally, we use salt or one of its chemical derivatives—soda, chlorine, or chlorine products—in many other ways, old and new.

For instance, salt is still an effective antiseptic. Gargling half a glass of warm water with a teaspoon of salt dissolved in it is a helpful home remedy for a sore throat. Salt is used in personal hygiene. Soda has long been used for cleaning teeth and has recently reappeared as a prime ingredient in certain popular toothpastes. Salt is used in making all kinds of food products, including canned foods, frozen vegetables, meats, even ice cream. Salt is also used in medicine. In hospitals, the first liquid delivered to patients through IV (intravenous) lines is saline solution, which is water sterilized with about 1 percent salt (sodium chloride). Salt plays a key role in our bodily health. The salt we digest in a well-balanced diet helps regulate our blood pressure, heart contractions, and nerve impulses (though excessive amounts may cause high blood pressure). And salt's contemporary usefulness doesn't end here.

Salt also plays a key role in public life. It is used in the construction of roads to provide more stable roadways. And in wintertime it is spread over snowy or icy roadways to help melt the wintry mix by reducing the temperature at which freezing occurs. Our tap water also has salt in it. According to one of the hydrologists at my city's water filtration plant, "1.5 parts per million" of the city's water is liquid chlorine, introduced solely as a disinfectant. A higher chlorine content (2 to 3 parts per million) keeps public and private swimming pools sufficiently germ-free for safe use. Salt is used in agriculture. To replenish their livestock's bodily salt content, ranchers and farmers graze their stock near salt deposits naturally exposed on the surface of their land (salt licks), or buy blocks of salt for their animals to lick, or mix salt with their feed. Some distribute salt in their stores of hay to help reduce moisture and prevent rot. And salt is even used in art. As described in chapter one, when stoneware receives its final firing, a large amount of salt is deposited directly into the blazing kiln to produce shining, "salt-glazed" pottery. Besides these, there are many other current industrial uses for salt and its chemical by-products.

In fact, it is estimated that over *fourteen thousand* industrial uses of salt, mostly from its chemical derivatives, exist today. Salt, soda, chlorine, or chlorine products are used in plants worldwide to make glass, soap, paper, petroleum products, steel, aluminum components, rubber tires, seat covers, paint removers, inks, dyes, pesticides, and thousands of other useful products. As if to underscore the point, while cleaning my computer keyboard today, I decided to check the active ingredients in the disinfectant cleaning fluid I was using. The first item listed was "sodium salt of o-phenylphenol," which was present in the small yet sufficient amount of 0.31 percent!

So there you have it. Salt is one of the most ubiquitous, accessible, valuable, and useful substances on earth.[5] And, yes, it's probably in your household cleaning fluids, too!

THE FIGURATIVE MEANINGS OF
"YE ARE THE SALT OF THE EARTH"

It's good to know that Jesus called Christians the "salt of the earth," and it's even better to know the facts about salt, but this isn't good enough. It is the spirit of the Word, not the letter, that gives fresh inspiration and life to our souls. So let's press on in our truth-search until we understand precisely and fully what Jesus was trying to say to *us* in His first similitude.

Used by Jesus as an analogy to our spiritual life, His words, "Ye are the salt of the earth," imply the following interpretations.

You are God's seasoning

Just as the presence of salt on otherwise tasteless meats makes them acceptable to our palates, so the presence of believers in human society makes this otherwise reprehensibly sinful race tolerable to a holy God. Until His plan of redemption runs its full course, the savor or taste of spiritual salt—Christ and His gospel truth, graces, and fruits in His people—enables God, for the time being, to accept this world as it is. Were it not for this planet's "seasoning" of believers, the Creator would utterly reject and swiftly judge humanity, as He did eons ago in Noah's day. (See Genesis 6:5–7.)

This sheds light on a key End-Time question. Many wonder, "When will the Rapture occur?" This similitude confirms that the Rapture of the church will occur *before* the tribulation period, because it will remove the salt of the earth, thus immediately making the world intolerable to God and inducing His manifest wrath in the form of unprecedented successful satanic deception and worldwide adversities (Rev. 6) and, in the latter half of that time, the terrible, terminal, earth-dismantling trumpet and bowl judgments (Rev. 8–11, 16). Such wrathful punishments could not occur if the salt of the earth were still present, seasoning the world to the heavenly Father's toleration.

Incidentally, the same holds for the second similitude, "Ye are the light of the world" (Matt. 5:14–16). The total spiritual darkness of the tribulation, which will include the worldwide worship of the devil incarnate and the full, unhindered proliferation of all forms of sin, *cannot* occur until the "light of the world" is removed. Hence, the removal of the church (and its Son-light) must precede the pitch-black night of Antichrist's rise and reign.

You are the world's preservative

The presence of salt on meat draws out its blood and water and, by osmosis, inhibits the growth of the resident bacteria that would otherwise cause rapid spoilage. Similarly, the mere presence of Christians in communities, cities, and nations inhibits the growth of sin in society, specifically, immorality, injustice, illegality, violence, war, and anarchy. Without "savory" Christians—strong believers filled with Christ's Spirit, truth, and grace—this world would soon corrupt, like raw meat exposed to the elements, and fall irretrievably into unrestrained immorality, violence, and anarchy. The Bible describes three such "saltless societies": the pre-flood world, Sodom, and the kingdom of Antichrist.

In Noah's day, when only eight salty souls inhabited the earth, all flesh was corrupted in a pandemic of sin. "The wickedness of man was great in the earth, and . . . every imagination of the thoughts of his heart was only evil continually" and the earth was "filled with violence" (Gen. 6:5, 13). Had the flood not occurred, the antediluvian world would have soon imploded through rampant violence, specifically murder. When only one righteous man, Lot, was present among the thousands of Sodomites, the city's wickedness became "great" and "very grievous" in God's sight (Gen. 18:20). Had fiery judgment not fallen on Sodom and its sister cities, the hellish spiritual wildfires of lust and greed would have soon burned up its terminally corrupt culture. And in Antichrist's reign, when only two salty prophets—God's "two witnesses" (Rev. 11:3)—will remain publicly visible and vocal for righteousness, the whole world will worship the devil incarnate. Yet even as the greatest overt judgments in history occur, the sinful majority will stubbornly refuse to repent of their corrupt living: "Neither repented they of their murders, nor of their sorceries, nor of their fornication, nor of their thefts" (Rev. 9:21). Thus the bacteria of sin *and* the plagues of God will combine to catastrophically dismantle the world's final sinful social order and earth's battered ecosystems.

Though sin is growing fast throughout the world today, it will not reach this outrageous apex until the "salt of the earth" (and the "light of the world"), the true body of fully committed believers in Jesus Christ, is physically removed through the Rapture. In the meantime, our very presence, along with our incessant intercessions and faithful witness, is preserving the present social order from the senseless self-destruction of sin.

You are the world's purifier

When used as an antiseptic, salt not only inhibits the growth of germs, but it also kills them! Thus, when salt is applied, cleansing or healing occurs; infection dies and purity of health is restored. When, as previously described, a city's water filtration plant applies liquid chlorine, a chemical derivative of salt, to its drinking water at a rate of 1.5 parts per million, its waters are disinfected, or "healed," of any dangerous microorganisms present. (See 2 Kings 2:19–22.) So salt and its chemical derivatives are *purifiers*. This characteristic of salt is also analogous to mature Christians.

Besides restraining the growth of sin in the larger populace, our presence, witness, and message of salvation and transformation through Christ both inhibit and kill sin in individual lives. Whenever the "salt" of God's Word and grace is received, spiritually defiled or impure souls are cleansed and made fit for God's fellowship, worship, and use. When Jesus met Zacchaeus, for instance, His strong savor arrested the corruption of greed in the notoriously defiled publican's heart; his healing was quickly apparent, as he began speaking truth and practicing generosity. A similar miracle of purification occurred years later when the apostle Paul came in direct, sustained contact with the thieving slave Onesimus. His wrongdoing was "disinfected" by the spiritually salty gospel message and life-example of Paul, who was himself a former persecutor of innocent

Christians and whose unbelief had been instantly purified by contact with earth's most salty One, its very mother lode of spiritual salt, Jesus, on the Damascus road. Onesimus' healing also was readily apparent, as he returned to his former master, Philemon, ready to serve, not steal.

And how many times since has the presence, personal witness, evangelistic message, corrective exhortation, or gentle mercies of a salty Christian purified a sinner's corrupt heart or a carnal Christian's lukewarm ways and caused them to soon thereafter manifest a new attitude, purity, purpose, and lifestyle? Why? Because their sins weren't just arrested; their souls were purified by contact with the salt of the earth.

You are the world's irritant

Systematic scientific research is not really necessary to discover that salt is a strong irritant to open wounds. The next time you scrape or cut yourself, cleanse the wound with heavily salted water, and no further experimentation will be necessary. You will immediately be convinced that salt irritates raw flesh. End of study.

Similarly, salty Christians filled with the Spirit and Word of Christ irritate people whose hearts are "raw" toward God due to unforsaken sin. Oswald Chambers said:

> To preserve from corruption, salt has to be placed in the midst of it, and before it can do its work it causes excessive irritation, which spells persecution [for the salty believer].

Perhaps this is why Jesus prophesied, "Ye shall be hated of all men for my name's sake" (Matt. 10:22), and "In the world ye shall have tribulation" (John 16:33). Or why He pronounced this strange blessing on us: "Blessed are ye, when men shall hate you, and . . . separate you from their company, and shall reproach you, and cast out your name as evil, for the Son of man's sake" (Luke 6:22). Or why He then instructed us, of all things, to "Rejoice ye in that day, and leap for joy; for, behold, your reward is great in heaven" (v. 23). But, specifically, why are we spiritual irritants?

Here are some reasons salty Christians sting certain people. Bible truth rightly presented irritates unbelievers, sinning Christians, and religiously deceived people. Godly living disgusts ungodly people. The most discreetly spoken witness concerning the new birth, the baptism with the Holy Spirit, the gifts of the Holy Spirit, the Second Coming, the judgments, and so forth elicits strong rejection from those who have been taught against these experiences or doctrines. Our claim that God wants us to be holy stirs contempt in those who prefer to indulge their carnal lusts. Our joyful hope in Jesus' appearing provokes hilarious mockery from those who deem it a biblical myth authored for the ignorant masses. Our choices to obey God shame those who stubbornly disobey Him. Our following of God's call rebukes those who have ignored or abandoned it. Our lives of devotion are despised by those who refuse to seek God. Our testimonies of answered prayer chafe those who prefer to depend upon reason alone in their troubles. Our boasting in God and failure to praise men excessively provoke those who praise men highly and fail to give God full credit. And in some cases, our mere physical presence causes the waters of resentment to rise and rivers of reproach to flow. Why? The salt of Christ in us is being applied directly to the raw flesh of fallen or redeemed but disobedient humanity. Have we accepted this calling?

It is important to note that this rejection for Christ's sake is *without* just cause; hence, it is *not* the kind caused by us speaking foolishly or unkindly, acting unfairly or arrogantly, doing things unethically or illegally, tending others' business, constantly badgering the unsaved about their souls, or trying to control people's actions without right. Jesus is neither pleased nor honored when we irritate people for these reasons.

We relish the thought of being holy intercessors, instructors, and inspirers, but are we ready to be holy irritants? Here is a true litmus test of our devotion to Jesus. Do we love Him enough to accept being rejected without a cause for His sake? If so, He will richly reward us one day. Indeed, the salty saints of this world will be the sure sovereigns of the next: "If we *suffer [for him]*, we shall also *reign with him*" (2 Tim. 2:12).

You are the world's judgment

The Bible repeatedly reveals that salt is associated with God's judgments. For instance, it is mentioned in the account of His judgment of the cities of Sodom and Gomorrah and their environs: "The whole land thereof is brimstone, and *salt* . . . like the overthrow of Sodom" (Deut. 29:23). It is most famously linked to His judgment

of Lot's wife, "his wife looked back . . . and she became a
pillar of salt" (Gen. 19:26). In the judgment of Shechem,
as mentioned earlier, salt is also mentioned: "And
Abimelech fought against the city . . . and *sowed it with
salt*" (Judg. 9:45). It is also referred to in His message of
judgment on the Judean apostates, "Cursed be the man
[men of Judah] that trusteth in man . . . he shall be like
the shrub in the desert . . . in *a salt land*, and not inhabited" (Jer. 17:5–6).

Lot's wife became a pillar of salt after she heard but
rejected God's Word of salvation in Sodom, which commanded her, "Escape for thy life; *look not behind thee*"
(Gen. 19:17). Similarly, the whole unbelieving world
will be judged for rejecting God's living Word of salvation, Jesus. And not only this, they will also be judged
for rejecting His messengers and the messages of salvation He gives them to speak. Jesus informed His original
spokesmen-disciples that it would be "more tolerable"
for the Sodomites at the judgment day than for the people who rejected His Word in their mouths: "Whosoever
shall not receive *you*, nor hear *your words* . . . *It shall be
more tolerable for the land of Sodom* and Gomorrah in the
day of judgment, than for that city" (Matt. 10:14–15).

Just as salt saves bodies from death by bacterial
invasion, so the salt of gospel truth saves souls from sin,
condemnation, and ultimate damnation—but not if it is
rejected. Have we realized that our presence, witness, and
message bring people to judgment, requiring them to
make pivotal decisions about unalterable, eternal truth:
the living Word and the written words of God? After
encountering the salt of the earth, whether in living or

literary form, in the Master or His messages, the people of earth are never the same. Some receive the salt and God's blessing; others reject it and receive His judgment. Have we given thought to this phase of our call?

Some people will be in heaven because, with the Spirit's leading and help, we spoke the salt of gospel truth to them: "Now, then, we are ambassadors for Christ, as though God did beseech you by us . . . be ye reconciled to God" (2 Cor. 5:20). Others will spend eternity in the horrible torments of hell because they stubbornly rejected us, the chosen messengers of the most salty One, and the life-giving words He gave us to speak. We play a similar role toward our fellow Christians.

Some Christians will enjoy a full, indescribably rich reward in New Jerusalem because they received the salt of our instruction, corrective counsel, or loving exhortation. Others will be without rewards because they rejected us and the corrective truth we spoke in love.

Like Israel's true prophets, then, Christ uses His true spokesmen-disciples to bring all people to a reckoning.

You are very useful to God and man

Just as salt is very useful to mankind publicly, hygienically, medicinally, artistically, and industrially, so also are strong Christians. Consider how we help the Creator and His creatures.

Publicly, or socially, we aid our communities, cities, and nations by being a stabilizing force. The best thing a mayor, governor, or head of state can have in his constituency is a large segment of strong Christians living lawfully, peacefully, lovingly, and productively. Hygienically, Christian evangelism, powered by the Holy Spirit through intercession, cleanses hearts, homes, and communities of otherwise highly infectious sins and causes of societal turbulence and decline. Steady, Spirit-led Bible teaching further disinfects those who are spiritually reborn, and, indirectly, the public atmosphere surrounding them. Medicinally, the marvelous healing ministry of Christ through the members of His body heals many people who are emotionally crushed, mentally disturbed, or physically ill. Economically, hard-working, dependable Christians build or sustain strong farms, vital businesses, and foundational industries, thus creating and sustaining a divinely blessed, stable, long-term economic growth not possible where atheism or false religions are the prevailing spiritual influence. And culturally, gifted Christians provide society with works of beauty artistically, musically, and literarily. For instance, John Bunyan is considered by many scholars to be the father of the novel due to the sheer beauty of language, colorful characters, and orderly progression of thought in his masterful allegory of the Christian life, *The Pilgrim's Progress*. Other examples are the revered and masterful musical compositions of Bach and Handel. And our usefulness doesn't end here.

To God, our primary usefulness lies in facilitating His grand plan of redemption, paid for by His Son's blood, and in calling, teaching, training, helping, and fellowshiping with those who will inhabit and/or rule His kingdom after His Son returns. In short, we are God's kingdom construction agents, the hands, tools, and human "machines" with which He is building His and our perpetual paradise, now as a spiritual or hidden realm (the church) in and among those who submit to Christ's lordship and, after Armageddon, as a visible, world-governing domain (the kingdom).

So the next time the devil tells you that you're not useful, tell him to "Get!"—then confidently inform him that you are just as useful as salt! In a plethora of practical ways, you are helping the creature, the Creator, and His present and perpetual kingdom!

God will scatter you all over the world

Everyone should agree that salt is a substance that is scattered everywhere. God has spread huge underground deposits of rock salt all over the world and sprinkled high concentrations of brine in all the oceans and even in lakes and springs. Not surprisingly, the creature has followed the Creator's example. Every day we scatter salt all over our food, and every winter we spread it all over our roads and sidewalks. Hence, sodium chloride is not concentrated in one place but rather disseminated throughout the world—just like potent Christians.

After Pentecost, it looked for a while as if the salt of the earth would remain concentrated in a single, solid deposit: the Jerusalem salt dome. But the master salt Shaker had already spoken: His gospel and its preachers and practitioners would be strewn all over the earth. "Ye shall be witnesses unto me . . . in Jerusalem . . . Judea . . . Samaria, *and unto the uttermost parts of the earth*" (Acts 1:8). And so it was. The Book of Acts confirms that, indeed, the people of the Way soon parted ways to carry word of the Way in every highway—north, south, east, and west. But how did this happen? The great "shaking" of the salt of the earth was facilitated by the commissions of God's Word, the calls of His Spirit, and, when necessary, conflicts with His enemies.

Initially, the living Word issued and the written Word recorded the preacher's commission, "Go ye into all the world, and *preach* the gospel to every creature" (Mark 16:15). And, as Matthew recalls it, the teacher's commission, "Go ye ... and *teach* all nations" (Matt. 28:19). So in obedience to these Messianic mandates, the apostles went forth to preach and teach their salty message.

Then the Spirit begin calling them to specific salt-distribution missions, "Separate me Barnabas and Saul for the work unto which I have called them" (Acts 13:2). So the first Christian missionaries went forth to tell others of the earth's most salty One.

Finally, God permitted the church's enemies to shake all the Jerusalem salt crystals from their preferred and comfortable residences: "At that time there was a great persecution against the church ... and *they were all scattered abroad*" (Acts 8:1). Wherever they went, the first believers took their spiritual salt—the gospel of the grace and truth of God—with them: "They that were scattered abroad went everywhere *preaching the word*" (v. 4). These events comprised the church's first great salt shaking. And God has continued down through the centuries to scatter His people. My native land, America, was well salted several centuries ago, chiefly with exceptionally committed Separatists from England and the Netherlands; Puritans from England; Calvinists from Switzerland and Scotland; Mennonites from Switzerland, Germany, and the Netherlands;

Huguenots from France; Lutherans and Moravians from Germany; and others.

So don't be surprised or afraid if God lays hold of your domestic, occupational, or ecclesiastical salt shaker, turns it upside down, and begins providentially scattering you or your believing friends or family—to new cities, nations, jobs, ministries, or missions. It's part of your destiny in Christ. The salt of the earth is made to be scattered, not settled. Besides, can't the sovereign, heavenly Shaker of salt who created and redeemed you disperse you as He wills? So don't resist the shaking; revel in it! And trust the Shaker. Wherever He flings His salt is where it is most useful. "Trust in the LORD with all thine heart, and lean not to thine own understanding. In all thy ways [circumstances] acknowledge him [his control and wise plan], and he shall direct thy paths [perfectly]" (Prov. 3:5–6).

You are as valuable as money

Historically, salt was so highly valued it was used as money. Men have desired it so ardently that they have made great sacrifices for it, including building roads to transport it, trading their prized silver or gold to obtain it, and facing deadly perils to extract it from mines deep in the earth.

In the same way, God considered His people to be so valuable He willingly gave up the best thing He had—His "gold" and heaven's fortune, His only begotten Son—to save, sanctify, and have us for His own. A bloody cross that stood long ago on a hill outside of Jerusalem is proof enough for any doubter. But it didn't end there.

Today God still values us so highly that He stands ready to do whatever is necessary to provide for us and protect us. Just as He sacrificed the oppressive Egyptians to save His oppressed Hebrew people, so He stands ready to do anything—confuse, divide, dispirit, deceive, defeat, even destroy—those who stubbornly oppose our work in Christ or cruelly and impenitently attack and persecute us and our loved ones.

He removed King Herod Agrippa I to prevent him from trying again to kill the apostle Peter as he had the leader of the Jerusalem church, James. He stunned and blinded Saul of Tarsus on the Damascus road rather than let him continue imprisoning and killing His precious children. He also struck Elymas the sorcerer temporarily blind so that the Roman governor, Sergius Paulus, could hear the gospel and receive the new birth. And He brought overwhelming judgment on the stubborn Christ-, gospel-, and church-rejecting Jews in A.D. 70 by permitting the Romans to utterly destroy Jerusalem and its precious temple and scatter the Jews to the four winds. All these defensive divine interventions reveal how highly God values "the salt of the earth."

So the next time you're in distress, remember how valuable you are to God—as valuable as salt was to the ancients! Then listen to His confirming, comforting promise: "Fear not . . . when thou passest through the waters, I will be with thee, and through the rivers, they shall not overflow thee; when thou walkest through the fire, thou shalt not be burned" (Isa. 43:1–2). And why? "For I am the LORD [and] . . . I gave Egypt for thy ransom. . . . *Since thou wast precious [lit. valued] in my sight . . . therefore will I give men for thee, and people for thy life"* (vv. 3–4).

Why not praise and thank your divine Defender right now in anticipation of His help? "When they began to sing and to praise, the Lord set an ambush against the children of Ammon" (2 Chron. 20:22).

You are a people of covenant

On the table at every covenant meal, salt was an indispensable part of ancient covenant making. The Arab expression, "There is salt between us," usually meant, "There is a covenant between us." A "covenant of salt" (2 Chron. 13:5) is a covenant as strong and enduring as salt. Hence, it speaks of an unchangeable, permanent agreement.

Like their mineral namesake, salty Christians live by and remain faithful to solemn agreements and unbreakable vows made before God and man. Before God we live in and under the terms of the New Covenant, the solemn saving and living arrangement God conceived and offered us through Christ's substitutionary sacrifice. Our covenant meal is the Lord's Supper. Every Christian who receives of the cup and the bread may and should say to God, "There is salt between us"—and then joyfully and devotedly live by the terms of that covenant, the New Testament. And before men, salty Christians gladly keep faith by abiding by the terms of their human covenants. If married, they live faithfully with their spouses. In their business affairs, they conscientiously observe the terms of their business contracts. In financial matters, they accept only those commitments they can honor, and they diligently honor the terms of those commitments. As citizens, they obey the "covenant" of their land, that is, its constitution, laws, regulations, and court orders. As tradesmen or professionals, they willingly observe the codes and ethics that regulate their trade or profession. As ministers, they faithfully pursue their primary New Covenant ministerial responsibility by giving themselves "continually to prayer, and to the ministry of the word" (Acts 6:4). And they also gladly obey the bylaws and regulations of any denominational or ministerial associations to which they may belong. Why? Because they are covenantal Christians. There is salt in them, there is salt between them and God, and there is salt between them and other people.

If we will not live in covenant with God and men now in this world, what makes us think we will live faithfully with the Savior and the saints in the next? Let us honestly search our hearts by asking, Are we covenant makers or "covenant breakers" (Rom. 1:31), that is, "conscienceless and faithless" (AMP)? Don't abandon your vows, pledges, and agreements. Rather, embrace them and delight in discharging them as unto Christ! Have salt in yourself! Be a covenantal Christian!

You are a hospitable people

Obviously, in ancient Middle Eastern culture people didn't share meals just to seal covenants. Their dinners were also occasions for hospitality. One source notes that to "eat salt with" a person was *to share his hospitality*. This, of course, would have been common knowledge in Jesus' day and culture. Hence, by using salt as a metaphor for His people He was saying, "You are a hospitable people." And to Christ's words in Matthew's Gospel the epistles add their loud and clear, "Amen."

The apostle Paul exhorted the Romans to be "given to hospitality" (Rom. 12:13). He taught Timothy that ministers should not hold office unless they too were "given to hospitality" (1 Tim. 3:2), and he urged Titus to follow the same guidelines: "A bishop [minister] must be . . . a lover of hospitality" (Tit. 1:7–8). The apostle Peter agreed that all believers should "use hospitality one to another without grudging" (1 Pet. 4:9). The apostle John commended Gaius' church for their hospitality to "the brethren, and to strangers" (3 John 5) and urged them to extend the same to traveling ministers: "If thou bring [ministers] forward on their journey after a godly sort, thou shalt do well . . . receive such, that we might be fellow helpers of the truth" (vv. 6–8). Jesus went so far as to promise a reward to anyone who gave even a "cup of cold water only" to one of His deeply committed student-followers (Matt. 10:42). He pledged even greater rewards to those who lodged His appointed messengers: "He that receiveth a prophet [into his home] in the name of a prophet shall receive a prophet's reward" (v. 41).

Not stopping there, He promised rewards to those who show hospitality to even "one" of His least committed, least worthy followers: "Inasmuch as ye have done it unto *one of the least* of these my brethren, ye have done it unto me" (Matt. 25:40). And, apparently with Abraham's noble example in mind (Gen. 18:1–8), the writer to the Hebrews reminded us that, because angels sometimes temporarily assume human form, we should even show hospitality to strangers, lest we unintentionally offend an angel: "Do not forget or neglect or refuse to extend hospitality to strangers [in the brotherhood—being friendly, cordial and gracious, sharing the comforts of your home and doing your part generously], for through it some have entertained angels without knowing it" (Heb. 13:2, AMP). But there is an exception to this.

In these unusually evil and perilous times, for instance, prayerful discretion should be exercised in choosing who to "entertain" and how far we should extend our hospitality. As if anticipating such crucial choices, the apostle Paul commanded us, "Walk in wisdom toward them that are outside," (Col. 4:5). Truly, we don't want to entertain any *fallen* angels unawares! Despite this exception, being hospitable is the rule.

So, as God gives you opportunity, offer the "salt" of hospitality freely, to friends, neighbors, visitors, and even to strangers. Encourage them to sit and talk a while and have something to drink and eat. Why? For love's sake, to be sure. But also to demonstrate to the most hospitable One that, truly, you are "the salt of the earth."

You are a people who make sacrifices for God and His kingdom

As stated earlier, under Mosaic law salt was included in all sacrifices. Numerous references underscore this example: "Neither shalt thou allow the salt of the covenant of thy God to be lacking from thy meal offering: with all thine offerings thou shalt offer *salt*" (Lev. 2:13). "Thou shalt offer a young bullock without blemish, and a ram . . . and the priests shall cast *salt* upon them" (Ezek. 43:23–24). (See also Ezra 6:9; 7:22.) And Jesus summarized this subject by saying, "Every sacrifice shall be salted with *salt*" (Mark 9:49). Hence God's Word makes a strong link between salt and sacrifices.

As the "salt of the earth," therefore, Christians are inextricably linked to the offering of sacrifices to God. By declaring, "Ye are the salt of the earth," Jesus was saying, "You are a people who make sacrifices for Me and My kingdom." What kind of sacrifices are these?

We offer the sacrifice of praise daily: "By him, therefore, let us offer the sacrifice of praise to God continually, that is, the fruit of our lips giving thanks to His name" (Heb. 13:15). (See 1 Thessalonians 5:18.) And when the need presents itself, we give our monies and materials sacrificially, as the early church did to support its poor and its foreign visitors: "And all that believed . . . sold their [extra] possessions and goods, and parted [the proceeds from the sale of] them to all men, as every man had need" (Acts 2:44–45). By bearing the crosses God lays upon us, we sacrifice our self-will in order to do Christ's will and, as His true disciples, spread His Word: "Lo, we have left all, and have followed thee" (Mark. 10:28; see v. 29; Luke 14:25–33.) And by enduring periodic persecutions, we sacrifice our comforts, good names, liberties, possessions, and, in extreme cases, bodies, to further Christ's truth and kingdom. The history of Christianity is filled with the sacrifices of the saints; from the Jewish to the Roman to the Medieval persecutions, to those of the great Reformation and all the revivals that have followed, brave and uncompromisingly righteous believers have paid dearly for reforming their churches or reviving their fellow believers. Why? Because they possessed spiritual salt—the grace to suffer willingly for Christ's Word, plan, and kingdom. The original apostles had this salt in them: "And they departed . . . rejoicing that they were counted worthy to suffer shame for his sake" (Acts 5:41). So did Paul, who wrote, "I will very gladly spend and be spent for you; though the more abundantly I love you, the less I be loved" (2 Cor. 12:15).

Do we have this kind of salt in us today? Time, tests, and troublemakers will tell. All who hold to biblical truth and righteous living in this final, lukewarm, "Laodicean" period of the Church Age will suffer some form of rejection from today's spiritually saltless societies and savorless churches: "Yea, and all that will live godly in Christ Jesus shall suffer persecution [persisting rejection, ostracism, harassment, injustice, indignities, injuries]" (2 Tim. 3:12). Will we go through with our personal sacrifices or go back? If we go through with them, Jesus has assured us that He will abundantly repay us one day on this earth: "There is no man that hath left house, or brethren, or sisters, or father, or mother, or wife, or children, or lands, for my sake, and the gospel's, but he shall receive an hundredfold [that is, many times more than what he sacrificed] now in this time . . ." (Mark 10:29–30).

You are a people of gracious speech

One isolated New Testament reference makes an unmistakable connection between salt and gracious speech:

"Let your speech be always *with grace,* seasoned *with salt*" (Col. 4:6). Note that speech "with grace" is speech that has been seasoned "with salt." The gifted Assemblies of God teacher Walter Beuttler noted, "Salt . . . speaks of the divine grace in Christ which made his life savory to both God and man."[6] This grace was especially evident in the gracious words that flowed from the Master's tongue.

Foreseeing Christ's uniquely winsome words, the psalmist wrote, "Thou art fairer than the children of men; *grace is poured into thy lips*" (Ps. 45:2). Luke confirms a fulfillment of this prophecy in Jesus' ministry in Nazareth: "And all bore him witness, and wondered at the gracious words which proceeded out of his mouth" (Luke 4:22). The sheer beauty of Christ's words arrested many: "Never man spoke like this man" (John 7:46). Their convicting quality was unmatched: "He that is without sin among you, let him first cast a stone at her" (John 8:7; see v. 9). Their timeliness was exquisite. Their boldness was inspiring. Their gentleness was most endearing. Their biblical content was undeniable: "But he answered and said, It is written . . . It is written . . . It is written" (Matt. 4:4, 7, 10). Even Christ's discreetly chosen moments of silence evinced an otherworldly grace and wisdom: "But Jesus stooped down, and with his finger wrote on the ground, as though he heard them not" (John 8:6). And it is with this, His grace, "the divine grace in Christ," that we are commanded to speak: "Let *your speech* be always with grace . . . with salt" (Col. 4:6).

Many honest Christians may think or say, "That's impossible! I can't speak with the grace of Christ." These sincere but doubting Thomases have forgotten two key biblical truths:

1. God has commanded us to speak graciously, and He never commands us to do what we can't do—all His commands are our enablings.
2. God's Word demonstrates that He is able to reproduce Jesus' gracious speech in the ungracious sons of Adam.

Stephen is a case in point. When his religious enemies viciously contended with him, Stephen responded with such God-given confidence and grace that "they were not able to resist the wisdom and the Spirit [Holy Spirit and the bold yet civil spirit He imparts] by which he spoke" (Acts 6:10).

So in obedience and faith let's commit ourselves to learn to speak always "with grace . . . with salt." Henceforth, may our words be deliciously salted with Christ's words and with His patience, discreetness, gentleness, mercy, frankness, and boldness! And may we learn to walk so closely with Him through the day that, truly, *He* speaks through us, as He spoke through David! "David, the son of Jesse, said . . . *The Spirit of the* LORD *spoke by me*, and *his* word was in *my* tongue" (2 Sam. 23:1–2).

You are a people of peace

In the Gospel of Mark, Jesus said, "Have salt in yourselves, and have peace one with another" (Mark 9:50). Thus He associated salt with peace: "Have salt . . . have peace." If we have salt in ourselves, spiritually speaking, we will have peace both in ourselves and with one another: "in yourselves . . . one with another." So by declaring, "Ye are the salt of the earth," Jesus was saying, "You are a people of peace."

Indeed, the Christian should be the most peaceful of men. Why? Because in Christ we have what sinners have not, "peace with God" (Rom. 5:1), by which we receive and live in the "peace of God" (Phil. 4:7). It is this spiritual salt of inner peace—a core tranquility, rest, contentment, and freedom from agitation—that makes us peace-loving, peace-making, and peace-propagating people. That is, we delight in calmness and despise contention; our words and actions destroy unnecessary, fruitless divisions and restore fruitful unity; and our exhortations and examples inspire others to become peacemakers. All this peace is derived from the pure salt of God's Word. Like a powerful antiseptic, when received, it kills the agents of agitation.

For example, the Word commands us not to covet: "Thou shalt not covet . . . anything" (Exod. 20:17). Instead, we are to be content with what we have: "Be content with such things as ye have" (Heb. 13:5). It forbids us to be contentious: "Strive not about words to no profit. . . . The servant of the Lord must not strive" (2 Tim. 2:14, 24). Instead it recommends gentleness and patience: " . . . must . . . be gentle unto all men, apt to teach, patient" (v. 24). It points us away from selfish and futile worldly strifes by instructing us to set our thoughts and desires on "things above, not on things on the earth" (Col. 3:2). God's Word also commands us not to exacerbate but to extinguish petty divisions: "Be at peace among yourselves" (1 Thess. 5:13).

If we do these things, we will possess the potent "peace of God, which passeth all understanding" (Phil. 4:7). And our lives will be pleasing responses to God's call for peace, for "God hath called us to peace" (1 Cor. 7:15). We will be living answers to Paul's many invocations for peace: "Grace to you and peace from God" (Rom. 1:7). (See 1 Corinthians 1:3; 2 Corinthians 1:2; Galatians 1:3.) Then wherever we go, we will scatter the salt of peace, always preserving or restoring, and never disturbing, the serenity of God's order.

There is only one scenario in which salty Christians will acquiesce in division, that is, when God ordains special tests of opposition for our spiritual growth. These spiritual "wars" occur when in some way our adversaries demand we turn from God's will—by denying our Savior or His Word, or by abandoning His high standards of righteousness, the study of His Word, the pursuit of His calling, obedience to His guidance, or our worship and fellowship with other committed Christians. Whenever unreasonable people loudly demand (or quietly but persistently request) that we give up these things "or else," we must give thanks to God and willingly embrace the "or else," however uncomfortable, as the cross He has given us. While peace with God and the peace of God are always easily within our reach, peace with all people is not. Hence Paul wrote, "*If it be possible*, as much as lieth in you, live peaceably with all men" (Rom. 12:18). Salty saints accept the fact that peace is sometimes impossible for the present. Have we learned this vital lesson yet?

Never compromise or abandon God's Word or will in your life to save any friendship. Such a union will be unreal

(2 Cor. 6:14–17) and its peace false, unsatisfying, and temporary. (And it will be dangerous. King Jehoshaphat learned just how perilous it is to make peace with known enemies of God. You can read about this in 2 Chronicles 18:1–34; 19:1–2!) As much as Luther initially wanted peace with Pope Leo X and his prelates so that the Roman church could be cleansed and restored to biblical conformity, he would not deny his teachings, which were founded in the inerrant Word of God, in order to have it. Why? Luther was a man of salt. He would not abandon the salt of God's truth to have the savor of false peace.

Are we strife-makers or peacemakers? Do we stir and prefer contention or camaraderie? Do we enjoy peace with God and with men, or is something disturbing our peace with God and ruining our ability to live in His peace among men? And are we willing to forgo peace with men, if necessary, to retain peace with God? There is salt in these truths; let's savor it.

God will extract you from the earth one day

What good could salt do us in this world if it was never extracted from the earth or its waters? Hence men assiduously remove the natural salt of the earth, by either mining or evaporation, so they can use it. And what good would Christians, the spiritual "salt of the earth," be to God in eternity if He did not one day extract us from this world?

As with sodium chloride, our extraction is sure, though its method varies. Some of us will leave this world by way of natural death. Others will remain alive until Jesus appears to catch us away unto Himself. When

Extraction Day comes, all "the salt of the earth," both living and dead, will be suddenly, supernaturally harvested in the twinkling of an eye to be "ever ... with the Lord" (1 Thess. 4:17) (See 1 Thessalonians 4:13–18; 1 Corinthians 15:51–53.) How may we be sure of this?

There are at least four reasons every salty Christian may be confident of eternal extraction: divine prayer, divine promise, divine prophecy, and divine planning.

First, Jesus prayed for our extraction from this world: "Father, I will that they also, whom thou hast given me, be *with me where I am [in heaven] ... [and] behold my glory*" (John 17:24). Without this request in His high priestly prayer, there would be no Rapture. Second, He plainly promised to return and extract us: "If I go and prepare a place for you [in heaven], *I will come again, and receive you unto myself,* that where I am [in heaven], there ye may be also" (John 14:3). God does everything by promise, and once Jesus gave this promise, He became pledge-bound to one day "receive us unto himself." Third, the prophecies of the New Testament unmistakably foretell of the great catching up of the salt of the earth: "The Lord himself shall descend from heaven ... and the dead in Christ shall rise first; then *we who are alive and remain shall be caught up together with them ... to meet the Lord in the air*" (1 Thess. 4:16-17). And what is written in His Word, God will never "write off," that is, forget or cancel, for "the scripture cannot be broken" (John 10:35). Fourth, it is God's plan to at some point remove the salt of the earth, for only then can the events of the tribulation period unfold. As mentioned earlier, if we are God's seasoning and the world's purifier and preservative from corruption, how can the divinely predestined End-Time story—of a world utterly corrupted with Antichrist worship and unchecked wickedness—unfold with the salt of the earth still present? Clearly, it can't. So we conclude that the extraction of all God's purifying agents, including the Holy Spirit who indwells them, must precede the rise and reign of the man and kingdom of corruption. "He [the Holy Spirit and the true church He indwells] who now hindereth [the rise and reign of Antichrist] will continue to hinder until he be taken out of the way. And then shall that wicked one [Antichrist] be revealed" (2 Thess. 2:7–8).

Friend, are you ready for extraction? If so, fine; stay salty. If not, identify and eliminate whatever has caused you to lose your "savor," or spiritual strength and desire derived from your closeness to Christ, fullness of His Spirit, and righteousness of life. Why? Because Jesus hasn't promised to extract savorless salt.

JESUS' CRUCIAL CLARIFYING COMMENTS

Having reviewed the figurative meanings of Jesus' declaration, let's consider the very important additional comments He made to help us interpret His declaration accurately. After declaring, "Ye are the salt of the earth," our Lord went on to say:

> *But if the salt have lost its savor,* with what shall it be salted? It is thereafter good for nothing, but to be cast out, and to be trodden under foot of men.
> —MATTHEW 5:13

With this fuller description in mind, we may paraphrase Jesus' declaration as:

You are the salt of the earth—but not all of you!

Thus He really described not one but *two kinds of salt.* One has retained its savor; the other has "lost its savor." One is good for use; the other is "good for nothing." One is kept and highly valued by God and men; the other is "cast out" as worthless. One is honored by God and good men; the other is contemptuously "trodden under foot of men." (See John 15:6; 1 Corinthians 9:27.)

These two kinds of salt describe two kinds of Christians, spiritual and carnal Christians respectively. Hence we conclude that *the figurative meanings opened above apply only to Christians who maintain their "savor."*

This begs three questions: What is our "savor"? How do we maintain it? How do we lose it?

What is our "savor"?

Salt's "savor," or sodium chloride content and salty taste, is determined by its purity. Table-quality salt is about 97.5 percent pure sodium chloride. As admixture with other minerals and substances increases, salt loses its "savor," or purity, potency, and salty taste, and consequently its effectiveness as a seasoning.

Hence, our spiritual "savor" is our spiritual purity or potency. This saltiness may be measured by any one of these similar yet separate tests: by our fullness of the Holy Spirit; by our closeness to Jesus; by our delight in and obedience to God's Word; by the intensity of our love for God and the reality of our compassion for men; by our adherence to God's ways of living and working; by our faithfulness in labor; by our endurance in suffering; by our dedication to God's call; by our willingness to receive God's correction, however sent; by our practical righteousness, or upright living; by our desire for Christ's holiness, or biblical purity in thought, word, and deed; by our lack of fascination with purely worldly interests, fads, and goals; and by the strength of our hope in Jesus' appearing.

How salty are you at present?

How do we maintain our "savor"?

Generally speaking, we maintain our "savor" by looking after our relationship to God "first," before all other responsibilities and interests, however necessary or admirable: "Seek ye *first* [to nurture and build] the kingdom of God [within you], and his righteousness" (Matt. 6:33).

Specifically, this means we seek God "first" every morning, feeding on His Word, praying, and worshiping before doing other things. In every situation daily, we first "give thanks" to God (1 Thess. 5:18), then trust and obey His Word or promptings. We put God first in relationships, turning away from sin and those who practice it and turning to others who are living righteously. We put God's truthfulness first, confessing our sins quickly and thoroughly and abiding consistently in the light of full honesty before God. We put the fear of the Lord first, choosing to stand in awe of Him and refusing to be overawed or intimidated by anyone. We put God's guidance first, trustingly following the direction of His Holy Spirit, even when we don't understand the way, or the end toward which, He is leading. We put God's chastening first, humbly receiving our heavenly Father's correction, whether through His Word, voice, counselors, or instructive interventions, and quickly changing our ways to please Him. We put God first in our finances, giving His tithes promptly and our offerings cheerfully. We put God first in our viewpoint, accepting all our crosses from Him and looking prayerfully for divine purposes in diabolical persecutions. We put God first in our worship, worshiping by choice, not feeling, and learning to always *refuse* to be offended with Him who is always good.

As we do these things, by God's grace we build and maintain a savory, or spiritually potent, Christian life.

How do we lose our "savor"?

The answer to this question is simple. We lose our "savor" by refusing or failing to discipline ourselves to live in the simple ways of God as described above. Thus by simply *not* strengthening our "savor," we gradually squander it. And soon the signs of spiritual dissipation begin manifesting in our living.

We lose our invigorating "first love" (Rev. 2:4), our trust in God grows weak, and our morals grow lukewarm and lax. Our obedience becomes sporadic, our discernment blurry, and our ears dull. Then our hope in God's promises, prophecies, and power withers and dies. Before long the world excites us and the Word bores us. We abandon our quest to know and do God's will and begin living again only for prosperity, pleasure, or play. Eventually our saltiness—potent faith, hope, love, zeal, and faithfulness in service—dissipates, and we resume full blown self-centered living. And our Lord is disappointed. Why? Because when we could have become "the salt of the earth," we persistently preferred to be "good for nothing" but to be "cast out" and "trodden under foot of men." Consequently, though the Lord wants to, He can't use us now. So He reluctantly sets us aside from His work and with grief permits us to be reproached by men, not for our holiness, but for our hypocrisy; not for our commitment, but for our carnality. And that's not the worst of it.

When that great "Extraction Day" comes, we'll be left behind. And when we cry out in protest, the earth's most salty One will say to us, "Verily I say unto you, I know you not [intimately]" (Matt. 25:12). If this dreadful specter doesn't spur us to build and maintain our savor, nothing will.

Now that you know the figurative meanings of Jesus' declaration, "Ye are the salt of the earth," and His crucial clarifying comments, let me—no, let God's Spirit—probe you. How does your spiritual life "taste" to God, my friend? Are you gaining or losing "savor" with each new day?

From now on, keep a close watch on your "savor." Fully do God's will by being "the salt of the earth"—and a modern day Magi.

Chapter Four

NEW TESTAMENT WISE MEN

Behold, there came wise men from the east to Jerusalem.

—MATTHEW 2:1

*T*HE OLD TESTAMENT describes wise men and women in no short supply. Ahithophel's counsel was as if God had spoken. King Solomon spoke thousands of insightful proverbs. Abigail had excellent understanding and prophetic vision. Daniel was a sage of unsurpassed wisdom. Joseph's interpretations were divine and unerring. Job's instruction strengthened many. And we could go on.

To this honorable catalog of wisdom, the New Testament adds its own wise ones. The apostle Paul was a brilliant leader, scholar, writer, and prophet. John was an inspired revelator and eloquent evangelist. Apollos was a man of learning and mighty in the Scriptures. Anna was a highly attuned and sensitive prophetess of God. And this list, too, we could extend considerably.

Not to be omitted from any biblical directory of shining ones are the wise men who visited the infant Jesus: "Behold, there came wise men from the east to Jerusalem" (Matt. 2:1). The facts given concerning these extraordinary Magi illustrate key characteristics of New Testament wise men, or wise Christian disciples. Let's consider them.

NEW TESTAMENT WISE MEN

While Old Testament wise ones are usually distinguished by their fear of God, good judgment, integrity, or by their spiritual and intellectual gifts, Matthew's Gospel reveals some additional traits by which we may distinguish wise men and women. Let's consider these characteristics of New Testament wise men as they appear in the experiences of the Magi recorded in Matthew 2:1–12.

Wise men seek Jesus diligently

The distant origin of these wise men reveals the depth of their desire to find and know God. Matthew says only that they came to Jerusalem from the east: "Behold, there came wise men *from the east*" (Matt. 2:1). Exactly from what Oriental nation or region they came is not disclosed. For all we know they may have come from as near as Assyria or as far as India or beyond. The language used suggests, but does not state, that they were from Iran. "Wise men" is translated from the Greek word *magoi*, which describes Persian sages who were expert in the study, and no doubt worship, of the stars. Could they have come from Persia?

We don't know where their epic journey began or how long it took, only that the star signaling the time of Jesus' birth originally appeared to them two years earlier. (See Matthew 2:7, 16.) Whatever their departure point, their quest represented a considerable effort and probably took a period of several months to a year or perhaps more. They made notable personal sacrifices, leaving behind their friends, family, and country; that much we know. And they persevered—likely enduring desert heat, windswept plains, rugged mountains, deep valleys, and rushing rivers, and risking vicious perils such as sandstorms and thieves—not stopping until they were in Jesus' presence: "And when they were come into the house, they saw the young child" (v. 11). To complete such an ambitious expedition demanded both determination and diligence. So whatever else is uncertain, it is certain that the wise men sought Jesus diligently. And it is equally clear that God noticed and rewarded their diligence by giving them their heart's desire. He led them straight to Jesus and permitted them to worship joyfully in His immediate presence.

Today God is searching for Christians who, like the wise men, are diligently searching for a greater knowledge of Him: "The LORD looked down from heaven . . . to see if there were any that did understand [that God exists], and seek God" (Ps. 14:2). Will we arrest His attention and garner His rewards as these Magi did? Will we by private prayer, Bible study, and worship seek Jesus Christ diligently—that is, with desire, regularity, and as our greatest necessity in life? Will we seek Him "first" every morning and make His will our "first" priority in every decision? "Seek ye *first* the kingdom of God [and its King], and his righteousness [righteous will]" (Matt. 6:33). If so, we will rediscover the truth the wise men discovered, namely, that, "he is a rewarder of them that diligently seek him" (Heb. 11:6).

And like these ancient Magi, our quest to draw near to and intimately know the King of the Jews will end in blissful success. God will give us our heart's desire— extraordinary closeness to Jesus. Every day we will look upon His face and read His heart's desires in Scripture, listen to His voice in prayer, marvel at His hand in our circumstances, and revel in the pure ecstasy of worshiping at His feet. There we will rediscover in our daily experience what the psalmist exclaimed long ago: "In thy presence is fullness of joy" (Ps. 16:11).

Wise men worship Jesus above all

Whatever their previous astrological beliefs, the wise men now worshiped Jesus above all other purported deities. Their stated purpose in coming was "to worship *him*"

(Matt. 2:2). They did not seek to worship the unique and fascinating star that signaled His birth, the famous king who gave them directions to His birthplace, the favored nation over whom He was destined to rule, or the chosen woman who gave Him birth. When in the house with Mary and Jesus, the wise men worshiped Jesus, not Mary. "When they were come into the house, they saw the young child with Mary, his mother, and fell down, and *worshiped him*" (v. 11). And all their gifts (worshipful sacrifices) were exclusively for Him, not for Mary, Herod, or the nation of Israel: "they presented *unto him* gifts" (v. 11). If they were merely scholars or typical astrologers and not true believers, they would have visited and viewed but not worshiped Jesus. But the Magi were more than intellectually curious about Jesus; they were internally captivated by Him. Indeed they had a measure of real faith in the only true God and were convinced that the child before them was His Anointed One: "Where is he that is born King of the Jews?" (v. 2). Thus their actions proved they were converted, not common, astrologers. Their study of the heavenly bodies may have continued, but their worship of them was forever eclipsed by the brilliant Morning Star.

Can the same be said of us? Are we worshiping only one "bright and morning star" (Rev. 22:16), or are we distracted by the deceptive and competitive glows of other bright lights in the religious galaxy? Many professing Christians unduly exalt, and thus worship, Mary or the saints, praying to them in lieu of the heavenly Father or Christ, our only Mediator (1 Tim. 2:5). Or they venerate the papacy, asserting that the Bishop of Rome is the head of the church and infallible when speaking in his official capacity, though the scriptures plainly assign those honors to Christ alone. Other Christians are entangled in astrology, worshiping literal stars by crediting them with guiding their lives. Still others are infatuated with "king worship," forever looking for and lauding "Herods," powerful, prosperous, or prestigious heads of state—whatever their religion. And some are so enamored with nationalism that they can see little else beside the passing glory of their native land, forgetful of the greater kingdom to which they have been called.

If we have set aside all these modern-day idols, however traditional, popular, or novel, and fixed our praise on Him in whom dwells "all the fullness of the Godhead bodily" (Col. 2:9), we are becoming New Testament wise men. We're worshiping God the Father in the Person of His Son by the inspiration of His Spirit—and no other!

Wise men receive and follow all forms of divine guidance

Wisely, the Magi perceived and followed all forms of divine guidance, natural and supernatural.

Naturally, or providentially, God guided them through the Jewish scribes, who taught them the prophecy pinpointing Bethlehem as the birthplace of Christ: "And they [the scribes] said . . . thus it is written by the prophet, And thou Bethlehem . . . out of thee shall come a Governor that shall rule my people, Israel" (Matt. 2:5–6). Because the substance of the scribes' counsel was the Scripture, God also guided the wise men through

His Word. He further guided them through the orders of the resident human authority, King Herod the Great, even though his character was reprehensible and sinister: "And he [Herod] sent them to Bethlehem . . . Go and search diligently for the young child; and when ye have found him, bring me word again, that I may come and worship him also" (v. 8). By complying with these naturally encountered initiatives and authorities, the wise men cooperated with God's providential guiding hand. But that wasn't all.

No mere rationalists, they also recognized and responded to God's supernatural guidance. When the star first appeared marking Christ's birth, they realized its significance and subsequently planned and launched their expedition to travel to the general area of Palestine (Matt. 2:1–2). When it unexpectedly reappeared and "went before them" (v. 9) in a miraculous intervention reminiscent of Israel's guidance by cloud in the wilderness (Num. 9:17–23), they again followed the star, this time to the exact city and house where Jesus lived (vv. 10–11). (By its irregular actions and location well *within* earth's atmosphere at an altitude low enough to indicate the very house Jesus was in, it is evident that this "star" was in every way extraordinary—a divinely created supernatural phenomenon, not any naturally occurring celestial star or body.) Also, when God warned them in a dream to flee from Herod rather than return to him, they promptly obeyed: "They departed into their own country another way" (v. 12). Thus God guided them by, and they responded to, His supernatural communications and indicators.

Are we wisely following or foolishly disregarding the various kinds of guidance God offers us?

When Naomi instructed Ruth as to how she should honorably propose a levirate marriage to Boaz, Ruth wisely obeyed (Ruth 3:5–6). Do we actually obey, or merely consider, discuss, and dismiss, the biblical principles and practical instructions our teachers offer us?

It was Joseph's obedience to Caesar's tax registration decree, which was motivated mostly by royal greed, that brought him with his espoused wife, Mary, to Bethlehem the very day Mary went into labor. Without Joseph's obedience to this imperial edict, Jesus would have been born, not in Bethlehem where the prophets had foreseen the blessed event, but in Nazareth where Joseph and Mary previously and subsequently resided (Luke 2: 4, 39). Do we obey the directives of our governmental authorities, even when they appear to be selfishly motivated?

It was Mary and Joseph's obedience to the Old Testament command to present and offer sacrifice for every newborn child that put them in touch with Simeon and Anna in the temple. Their subsequent prophetic comments ministered deeply to the new parents, giving them understanding for the perplexing years that followed. Do we obey all the applicable truths and commands we discover in the Bible, realizing that God's wise and benevolent guidance is inherent in His Word? Do we understand that to follow the letter of the written Word is to follow the will of the living Word?

It was Joseph's immediate obedience to the dream God gave him that protected the Christ-child from Herod's fury (Matt. 2:13–14). If the apostle Paul had not complied with his inspired dream in Troas, he would have never founded a key church in Philippi, which later served God honorably and supported Paul faithfully (Acts 16:9–15). Do we recognize and respond to dreams when it becomes clear to us that they are from God?

Wise men rejoice over God's guidance

When after some two years' absence the guiding star reappeared, the wise men were elated with "exceedingly great joy" (Matt. 2:10)—or "indescribable joy" (PHILLIPS) or "ecstatic joy" (AMP). Why? Because they realized how wonderful God was to show them the right way to His Son . . . again!

Are we equally appreciative of and thrilled by divine guidance? When we turn a corner and realize God has been leading us perfectly—ever closer to His Son and farther in His will—amid seemingly out-of-control, topsy-turvy, chaotic events, are we filled with "exceedingly great joy"? Do we bother to get alone with the Lord and lovingly bless Him for His precious personal guidance? Abraham's servant did so when he realized that the Lord had led him straight to the wife He had chosen for Isaac: "And the man bowed down his head, and worshiped. . . . *Blessed be the* LORD *God of my master* . . . I being in the way, *the* LORD *led me*" (Gen. 24:26–27). Do we do this haphazardly or habitually, in only some or in "all" the situations in which we detect His guiding hand? "In *all* thy ways [situations], acknowledge him [worshipfully credit God's control and acknowledge His presence and wise, loving plan]" (Prov. 3:6). Wise men do so—always.

After the Magi expressed their thankfulness for God's guiding star, God responded by sending them even more perfect guidance, this time a dream of warning: "*And being warned of God in a dream* that they should not return to Herod, they departed" (Matt. 2:12). What does this teach us? Simply that *appreciating divine guidance ensures its continuance.*

Why not worshipfully rejoice today that the Lord has lovingly led you farther in His will and drawn you closer to His Son . . . again, just as He has done a thousand times before? Be a New Testament wise man and offer Him "the sacrifice of praise . . . that is, the fruit of our lips giving thanks to his name" (Heb. 13:15). Then expect more perfect guidance tomorrow.

God delivers wise men from crafty deceivers

On this occasion King Herod the Great was like a very large and deadly snake well hidden in the tall grass of Judea, who, despite his highly developed skills of fraudulence, failed to deceive, use, or harm the Magi. With Luciferian subtlety Herod feigned genuine interest in, and even adoration for, the Christ child: "Bring me word again, *that I may come and worship him also*" (Matt. 2:8). But omniscience detected his serpentine motive and movements and, as I noted earlier, alerted the wise men to the present danger: "They were divinely instructed and warned in a dream not to go back to Herod" (v. 12, AMP). Thus Herod's lethal plot was foiled. Why? Because God sees the secret schemes and dangers that even His most perceptive saints cannot see, and He faithfully warns them of every hidden snake and snare. In similar ways, He has saved numerous other wise men from crafty deceivers.

He gave King Solomon the right judicial strategy to expose a lying litigant (1 Kings 3:16–28). He used a little boy's eavesdropping to discover the Jews' plot to assassinate the apostle Paul (Acts 23:12–16). And He enabled Nehemiah to see through the Samaritans' deadly traps, lying threats, and false prophecies (Neh. 6:1–14). Are we wise enough to recognize that our powers of discovery are extremely limited and to trust only in God's limitless knowledge and unfailing faithfulness to alert us whenever the evil sons of craft try to deceive, use, or harm us? If we're simple enough to "trust in the LORD with all thine heart" (Prov. 3:5), He will be faithful enough to deliver us from every deceiver and his or her covert plans.

That is, unless it's our time to suffer for Christ's sake. As well laid as Judas' plans were, they succeeded only because it was God's time for Jesus to suffer His cross. Previous to that hour Jesus' consistent testimony had been, "My time [to suffer] is not yet come" (John 7:6), and He had discovered and circumvented many premature attempts to arrest and execute him. John described one such time in his gospel:

> Then took they up stones to cast at him; but Jesus hid himself, and went out of the temple, going through the midst of them, and so passed by.
> —JOHN 8:59

But on that dark eve in Gethsemane, Jesus testified to His betrayer, "This is your hour, and the power of darkness"

(Luke 22:53). And He said to Pilate, "Thou couldest have no power at all against me, except it were *given thee from above*" (John 19:11). These testimonies, along with Jesus' thrice-repeated references to His betrayal and His giving of the sop to Judas, prove that He was privy to, not fooled by, Judas' plot—which unfolded as he planned only because it was a necessary part of the heavenly Father's higher plan.

If we are faithful, we should expect nothing less than this kind of full disclosure from our all-knowing, ever-faithful, heavenly Father. Shall He hide from Abraham's children of faith the thing that He does? Never! When you face demonically crafty adversaries, like Herod, isn't it wonderful to know that you're relying on an unfailingly faithful God?

Wise men study God's stars

As stated earlier, previous to their pilgrimage the Magi were professional stargazers (also probably scholars and/ or priests) who spent considerable time, effort, and, no doubt, money in pondering and worshiping the fathomless mysteries of the innumerable celestial bodies. While their idolatrous astrological beliefs were clearly false, these ancient watchers were nevertheless pondering objects created and owned by God. David recognized God as the Creator: "When I consider *thy heavens, the work of thy fingers*, the moon and *the stars...*" (Ps. 8:3). The Magi devoted their lives to studying the works of God in the heavens. Figuratively speaking, we should do the same.

We should spend considerable time and effort studying the "stars" among God's redeemed ones. We should become well acquainted with the most shining servants in His eternal kingdom, His best and brightest light-bearers, whose inspired faith and uncompromising righteousness stand out in this dark world filled with the shadowy evils of unbelief, false religions, and spiritual and moral compromise. Enoch, Noah, Joseph, Moses, Joshua, Samuel, David, Hezekiah, and Daniel are just a few of God's "stars" shining in the galaxy of the Bible. If interested, we may study their biographies there.

In the Scriptures, we will discover the origin of God's "stars." Surprisingly, many came from very ordinary backgrounds. We may ponder their uncompromising righteousness. They consistently refused to alter their biblical beliefs or divine calls to gain, or avoid losing, wealth, respect, power, or protection. From the Scriptures we learn how God made them shine. As they meditated on His Word and obeyed it, His righteousness glowed in and through them to others. We also learn how He caused their lights to burn more brightly—by allowing them to suffer betrayal, injustice, hardship, and delay for His sake. As they continued trusting and obeying Him in their difficulties, He refined, focused, and increased their inner light. And we see how God ultimately rewarded them: He gave them exceptional wisdom, gifts, skills, favor, and honor, placing them in His biblical galaxy of light-bearers. There are also other historical spiritual "galaxies" filled with large and fascinating "stars" for us to ponder.

For instance, the "stars" in the "galaxy" of the Middle Ages, such as France's Peter Waldo, should capture our attention. Or those of pre-Reformation times, such as Bohemia's John Hus. Or those of the Reformation, such as Scotland's John Knox. Or those of the late Reformation period, such as the influential German Pietist Count Zinzendorf, leader of the Moravian Brethren, whose extraordinary prayers and brave emissaries impacted the world and launched the Protestant missionary movement. Or those who shined brightly in the great nineteenth-century American revivals, such as Charles G. Finney. Or those of the modern era of worldwide Pentecostalism, Evangelicalism, and, most recently, Charismaticism. God has shined brightly through these and other "stars" in each of these "galaxies" of the broader universe of the church. Have we pondered their lives and followed their shining examples in Christ?

If so, God will make us shine just as they did and one day honor us—or, more accurately, the work of His Spirit in us. The Morning Star Himself has promised, "If any man serve me, let him follow me; and . . . *him will my Father honor*" (John 12:26).

Wise men give Jesus their best and value Him above all their worldly treasures

Arriving at Jesus' home, the wise men immediately "opened their treasures" and "presented unto him gifts: gold, and frankincense, and myrrh" (Matt. 2:11). Thus the Spirit describes their gifts, which consisted of precious metals and spices, as being their "treasures." Why? Because gold was then what it is now—mankind's most coveted precious metal. Frankincense and myrrh were very expensive spices imported from Southern Arabia, so expensive that only kings or the very rich possessed them. (Tradition suggests the wise men were kings.) Thus the Magi willingly gave up their treasures—their very best things—to honor and serve Jesus. Their actions proved that they valued Him, the "Desire of All Nations" (Hag. 2:7, NKJV), above all their worldly treasures.

They were not alone in this grace. Other New Testament wise ones gave up their very best things for Jesus. Mary of Bethany broke her alabaster box of precious spikenard, a rose-colored perfumed ointment imported from northern India and worth a year's wages, and lavishly poured it out on Jesus to prepare Him for burial (Mark 14:3–9). Saul of Tarsus laid aside his promising career as an up-and-coming leader of the Pharisees to serve and honor his newly discovered Savior (Phil. 3:4–8). Peter, Andrew, James, and John all left their precious families and valuable, jointly owned fishing business to follow the Nazarene Carpenter's call (Mark 1:16–20). Yet some, like the rich young ruler, refused to give up their best things to follow the Lord and fulfill His call on their lives. Which example are we patterning our lives after today?

In those pivotal moments when God calls on us to set aside our worldly treasures—businesses, careers, inheritances, houses and lands, offices, friends, families—to answer His heavenly call, do we let go of them, hold on to them, or hedge? Only immediate compliance with His call to surrender our treasures will distinguish us as wise. Every other choice, however wise and self-serving it may seem, will prove foolishly dishonoring to God and self-opposing in the end, because Jesus taught that if we seek to save the elements of our natural life, we will ultimately lose them: "He that findeth his life shall lose it . . ." (Matt. 10:39).

Will we give Jesus our very best? That is, the best of our day, in spending the early mornings alone with Him? Or the best of our human admiration, in wholehearted worship for Him alone? Or the best of our financial resources, in giving tithes cheerfully and gifts freely? Or the best of our physical strength, in laboring long hours at secular or ministry vocations? Or the best of our mental powers, in pursuing biblical and other pertinent studies? Or the best of our passionate loyalty, in a willingness to suffer crosses joyfully for His cause and kingdom? If so, He will give us His very best, the wondrous manifestation of His permeatingly peaceful and incomparably precious presence: "He that loveth me . . . I will love him, and *I will manifest myself to him [or make the reality of my presence known to his bodily senses]*" (John 14:21). And one day, in His time and way, and probably when we have long forgotten it, He will add back the very treasures we abandoned to fully apprehend Him and His plans for our lives: "Verily I say unto you, There is no man that hath left . . . for my sake, and the gospel's, but *he shall receive an hundredfold now in this time*" (Mark 10:29–30).

God shares His secrets with wise men

There are three key truths that God disclosed to the Magi that were hidden from Israel's public—from even her religious leaders. First, He notified them of the time and nation of Jesus' birth: "We have seen his [the King of the Jews, or Israelites'] star in the east" (Matt. 2:2). Second, by the star's reappearance God led them to the precise town and house where Jesus was living: "Lo, the star . . . went before them, till it came and stood over where the young child was" (v. 9). Third, God showed them Herod's well-disguised murderous intentions and warned them not to return to him: "Being warned of God in a dream that they should not return to Herod" (v. 12). Thus they knew what others didn't know. Why? Because God shares His secrets with New Testament wise men—God-fearing, born-again disciples of Christ who study and emulate the godly characteristics of the Magi.

His reasons for doing so in this context were three-fold. First, the Magi feared Him. This is seen in their sacrificial pilgrimage, their obedience to divine guidance, and their indisputable worship of God's Son. "The secret of the LORD is with those who fear him" (Ps. 25:14), or "the LORD confides in those who fear him" (NIV). Second, they were rapidly becoming His servants and to a lesser degree His prophets (or chosen spokesmen; note they conveyed the good news of Jesus' birth to Herod and Israel). "Surely the Lord GOD will do nothing, but he revealeth his secret unto his servants, the prophets" (Amos 3:7). Third, by their complete obedience to His revealed will, they qualified for friendship relationship with God. Jesus taught, "Ye are my friends, if ye do whatever I command you" (John 15:14). Then He added that He (God) discloses His secrets to His friends: "I have called you friends; for all things that I have heard of my Father I have made known unto you" (v. 15). Are these three things true of us?

Do we truly fear, or stand in awe of, God? Are we serving Him or ourselves? Are we His fully obedient friends? If so, He will share with us secrets of joy, just as He told shepherds who were faithfully watching their flocks by night the joyous report that Jesus had been born in Bethlehem (Luke 2:8–11). And, ever faithful to the whole truth, He will also share with us secrets of judgment, just as He informed young Samuel of His impending judgment on Eli and his corrupt sons (1 Sam. 3:11–13). Why should we desire to know God's secrets?

Because God's secrets save lives and cause His plans to succeed. If the wise men had returned to Herod, he would have immediately murdered the Christ child, and this would have thwarted God's plan of redemption. Who knows how many lives may be saved from the destruction of sin and how many divine plans may succeed rather than fail if we receive, obey, and share the rich secrets of God's Word and the joyous revelations and sober warnings of His Holy Spirit?

Wise men's messages of truth disturb corrupt leaders and lukewarm children of God

Did the chosen people and their leader rejoice when they heard the wise men's wonderful report that the "King of the Jews" was born? To the contrary, both king and constituents were highly displeased: "When Herod [the Great], the king, had heard these things, *he was troubled, and all Jerusalem with him*" (Matt. 2:3). This reaction proves that Herod was corrupt and his people backslidden.

Herod the Great, who was committed to Roman appeasement, including the promotion of Hellenism and emperor worship, was of Edomite descent and neither a true Jew nor by any means a sincere believer in Jehovah.

And, though very influential, the renowned Pharisaic party and movement promoted outward religious ritual only, not inward spiritual reality—or real faith in, obedience to, and intimate fellowship with God. The rival Sadducean party, composed of rationalistic-minded, upper-class priests and high-ranking members of the Sanhedrin who opposed strict Pharisaic piety, was no better. And had the people of Jerusalem been right with God, they would have reacted with *delight*, not distress, at the report of His Son's birth, as did Simeon, Anna, and the shepherds. When Simeon realized the infant Jesus was the Messiah, "then took he him up in his arms, and *blessed God . . .* " (Luke 2:28). When Anna realized the same, the aged prophetess "gave thanks likewise unto the Lord, and spoke [admiringly] of him to all" (v. 38). And when the shepherds heard of Jesus' birth, they "returned, glorifying and praising God for all the things that they had heard" (v. 20). But, sadly, tragically, neither Herod nor the people of Jerusalem rejoiced. Why? He was dishonest, they were disobedient, and neither wanted to hear God's true voice anymore.

In the same way the truth-honoring messages of New Testament wise men sometimes irritate carnal or sinful Christian leaders and lukewarm congregants, who then mislabel God's wise, peace-loving messengers as fools or troublemakers. But this blind rejection is not without well-documented Old Testament era precedents. Israel's true prophets experienced this same treatment in periods of national apostasy. The corrupt princes of Judah characterized Jeremiah's inspired explanation of Jerusalem's siege as being false and treasonous and cruelly punished him. The spiritually blind king Ahab, whose ambitious promotion of Baal worship fatally troubled Israel, had the cheek to call Elijah, whom God sent to restore righteousness and peace, a troublemaker: "Ahab said unto him, Art thou he who troubleth Israel?" (1 Kings 18:17).

This was also the case with the godly Bible scholars, translators, and reformers God sent to awaken the sleeping Roman church of the Middle Ages. Luther's suggested reforms deeply troubled the corrupt Pope Leo X and elicited not holy commendations but hot denunciations from the incensed pontiff. William Tyndale's "message" to England, the first-ever printed translation of the New Testament in English vernacular, so troubled Bishop Tunstall of London that the furious prelate bought every copy he could get his hands on, not to distribute but to destroy them, which he promptly did!

Sometimes the opposition of dark-hearted clergymen to light-bearing wise men and women is so great that the latter have to flee for their physical safety. The Magi "departed into their own country another way" (Matt. 2:12). Why? Because it wasn't safe for them to return to the raging king whom their God and consciences would not permit them to help. Martin Luther was hidden in the Wartburg castle while the pope's agents roamed Germany hoping to arrest and execute him. Tyndale had to flee England and take refuge in Antwerp, Belgium. And Jewish and Gentile animosity to the apostle Paul's gospel forced him to flee numerous times: from Damascus (Acts 9:23–25), from Jerusalem (vv. 29–30), and from Ephesus (Acts 20:1).

Are we so committed to *truth* and the God of truth

that we will speak words that stun and shake before they save, and give messages that bring trouble before they bring triumph? Will we face personal rejection, vicious reproach, wrongful legal actions, and, if necessary, violence, in order to awaken this Laodicean generation to the whole counsel of God? If so, we are wise men indeed.

Wise men are willing to leave their country and travel far for Jesus

When they first arrived in Israel and began sharing the good news about Jesus, the Magi had just completed a long and arduous journey from their unspecified eastern homeland. Whether that was Persia (Iran), as suggested earlier, or India, or even China, is not known, but that their journey took from six months to as much as two years is likely, for Jesus was not over two years old when they arrived. This fact is clearly implied because after Herod inquired "diligently" as to the time the star originally appeared, he ordered that all the children of Bethlehem be slain "from two years old and under" (Matt. 2:7, 16). But the question we wish to consider next is why. Why did these Magi leave their beloved country and travel so far?

Two reasons are apparent. First, they journeyed to see and know Jesus. This is underscored by the inquiry they made upon arrival, "Where is *he* . . ." (Matt. 2:2), and also by the fact that they didn't stop inquiring or traveling until they found Jesus: "When they were come into the house, *they saw the young child*" (v. 11). Second, they journeyed to obey God's call. You or I may have been uninterested in and unmoved by the phenomenal star, but to these divinely susceptible astrologers, its appearance was God's non-audible yet arresting summons to come to His land and people to meet and worship His Son. Hence, they left their own country and gladly trekked to a faraway land.

In doing so they pioneered a royal path that countless divinely called missionaries have followed. William Carey, Hudson Taylor, David Livingstone, and many others have responded to similar heavenly summons to faraway places. They crossed wide continents, rough oceans, treacherous mountains, dense jungles, and dangerous racial, ethnic, religious, and tribal barriers to answer God's call to share the good news about Jesus and, ultimately, to see and know Him more intimately. Why are there not more radically committed foreign missionaries today?

If called to prepare for foreign missions, will we answer the heavenly summons? If so, we will demonstrate a loyalty distinctly higher than that typically seen "for king and country" or "for president and party," namely, that which is "for Christ and His kingdom." Every patriot and nation will one day yield allegiance to that consummate and perpetual sovereign state, *the kingdom of Jesus Christ*. By adhering to this higher loyalty now, placing their loyalty to Christ above their own country, comrades, and comfort, missionaries help hasten the day of Christ's return and reign. God bless them!

And if not called to foreign missions, will we answer the Spirit's call to "leave" our country and travel far for Jesus *in spirit*? Will we abandon our nationalistic pride (though not our love for our native land), and travel far in the inner journey of our soul to a new, distant, and rarely visited spiritual destination, the mature, spiritually minded attitude of the new man, which glories *only* in the coming kingdom of God on earth? If so, we will be true Jews with truly circumcised hearts: "He is not a Jew who is one outwardly.... He is a Jew who is one inwardly; and [whose] circumcision is that of the heart ... *whose praise is not of men, but of God"* (Rom. 2:28–29). "We are the circumcision, who worship God in the spirit, and rejoice [always and only] in Christ Jesus, and *have no confidence in the flesh [goodness, wisdom, strength, or works of fallen humanity or our carnal nature]"* (Phil. 3:3). And we will also prove that we are New Testament wise men.

With these godly characteristics of the Magi fresh in our minds, let us ask God to put into our hearts the hunger and courage we need to follow their footsteps. But, wait, something's happening!

Look, the Magi's star is shining ... again! "There shall come a Star out of Jacob" (Num. 24:17). Can you see it? Will you follow it—or, follow *Him?* "I, Jesus, have sent mine angel to testify unto you ... *I am ... the bright and morning star"* (Rev. 22:16). If so, He will lead you to God's true people and places of true worship. He will lead you to wise, godly Bible scholars who will feed your faith and knowledge of God. He will give you exceedingly great joy every time He reveals Himself to you anew. He will enable you to discern deceivers and warn you to avoid them. He will lead you perfectly, always, even in faraway places and long, dark nights of testing. And ultimately He will bring you into His very presence, "to meet the Lord in the air;

and so shall we ever be with the Lord" (1 Thess. 4:17). So follow the Morning Star today—falling in with the long line of New Testament wise men and women trekking toward the kingdom—and never turn away.

And don't be surprised if you see some very small but hardworking creatures leading the way.

Chapter Five

THE WISE WAYS OF ANTS

Go to the ant . . . consider her ways.

—PROVERBS 6:6

WO EXCEPTIONALLY WISE monarchs of the ancient world, King Solomon and King Agur (author of Proverbs 30), were fascinated by the exceptionally great wisdom of one of God's most incredibly small creatures—the ant. Divine wisdom moved them to urge us to consider the "exceedingly wise" (Prov. 30:24) ways of ants so that we may discover and adopt their wisdom: "Go to the ant . . . consider her ways [behavior patterns], and be wise" (Prov. 6:6).

Despite this emphatic divine directive, the Bible contains only two references to ants. Interestingly,

143

and by inspiration, both urge us to consider the same specific "way" of ant life—*how ants gather and store their food.*

> Consider her ways... [she] *provideth her food...*
> *and gathereth her food.*
> —PROVERBS 6:6, 8

> Little... but... exceedingly wise... the ants...
> *prepare their food* in the summer.
> —PROVERBS 30:24–25

Before we go further in obeying this biblical directive, let's review some basic information about these tiny but smart insects.

ANT FACTS

Entomologists tell us that ants, which are highly interactive with and dependent on each other, are considered social insects.[1] They live in well-organized communities called colonies, with each colony residing in its own home, or nest. Ant nests are usually located underground with large hardened mounds of excavated earth, or anthills, covering them above. Ants are very diverse. According to world-renowned authority Edward O. Wilson, there are presently about twelve thousand known species of ants.[2] They vary in both color (black, brown, red, yellow, and so on) and size (from one-twenty-fifth of an inch to one inch in length). Phenomenally strong, ants can lift from ten to fifty times their body weight! (Imagine a two-hundred-pound man able to lift ten thousand pounds!) Their social structure is rigid, a veritable caste system, with queen ants established as the undisputed rulers, female worker ants as the most populous and active class, and males, who live very briefly and whose only function is to impregnate young queens, assuming the lowest class of ant society. Ants' life expectancy also varies greatly, with queens living about ten years; workers, one to five years; and males, only a few weeks to a few months.

Ant reproduction is highly unusual. Once in their lifetimes, young queens and males, both winged, undergo a "mating flight," during which they fly at a high altitude and copulate in flight. After returning to the ground, both queens and males shed their wings. The queen, permanently impregnated, then establishes a new nest, where she begins gradually laying what over her lifetime will be thousands of eggs, all fertilized in the initial mating flight. From these eggs will emerge new workers, queens, and males. The males, meanwhile, wander off and soon die.

Ant nests vary greatly in size. Some nests are as small as two inches and hold a mere dozen ants. Others cover large fields, extend to depths of forty feet, produce huge anthills, and are occupied by millions of ants. (I remember standing beside anthills in Natal, South Africa, four to five feet high!) Highly organized, these underground neighborhoods, dug entirely by worker ants and connected throughout by passageways, have numerous chambers designed for specific uses. In a typical nest, there are chambers for the queens and their newly laid eggs; "nurseries" where worker ants care for eggs, and, as they develop, larvae and pupae; storage chambers for food, such as seeds; rest chambers (even ants rest!); new rooms, apparently for anticipated expansion; and, usually deepest in the nest, "winter quarters." But not all species of ants are subterranean. Some live above ground in specially constructed leaf nests, in dead logs, or in the limbs of living trees; others cling together in clusters (bivouacs) and hang nightly beneath logs or limbs.

The anatomy of an ant is interesting. An ant's body has three major divisions, the head, trunk, and metasoma (which includes the "gaster," or large, rear section). Six long, thin legs project from the sides of its trunk, and two large, segmented antennae project forward from its head. All of an ant's senses (touch, smell, hearing, taste) except sight are resident in its antennae. Its front beak-like jaws, or mandibles, have a vertical rather than horizontal opening and are used for digging and cutting, as well as for grasping, carrying, pulling, or tearing to pieces various objects, including other ants! Most species have two well-developed, compound eyes with which they can quickly detect movements, but only at close range. Some species, for instance, all army ants, are completely blind. An ant's gaster has either a stinger or a gland with which it releases poison into or upon those it attacks.

Ants are eccentric but effective communicators. They signal one another by tapping their gasters on the sides of their nests (if nesting in leaves or limbs). This sends vibrations throughout the nest, usually to call the colony to come gather food that has been discovered or to warn it of an impending attack by a hostile colony's worker ants. Some ants have a special stridulatory organ that enables them to make a buzzing or squeaking sound used for the same purposes. Ants also release different chemicals (pheromones) from their bodies, detectible to other ants by taste or smell, which mark trails from their nest entrances to the sites of newly discovered food sources. They discharge other chemicals that signal their nest mates of impending attacks by hostile ants or predators.

An interesting feature of ant behavior is their voluntary sharing of food. Ants live largely off of liquids that are derived from chewing solid foods. When sharing food, ants stand head to head while one ant regurgitates liquid food from its temporary "crop stomach" and releases it through its mouth to feed the other ant.

Ants can be mildly or martially hostile. As with most creatures, ant conflicts usually arise over food. Sometimes worker ants, also known as "soldier ants" when in a combative posture, merely shove or bully one another in an attempt to establish dominance and access food. At other times, large, violent wars are fought between entire colonies of ants, during which millions of ants are slaughtered and after which the victors usually raid the defeated colony's nest, eat its food stores, and, yes, cannibalize its eggs, larvae, and pupae.

These are just a few of the interesting facts and ways of the tiny beings who live and labor beneath our feet and thoughts—yet command the attention of God and fascinate the wise.

Now, in obedience to God's Word, let's consider more specifically how ants gather and store their food.

HOW ANTS GATHER AND STORE THEIR FOOD

In this chapter, we will focus on six kinds of ants: army ants, harvester ants, dairying ants, honey ants, fungus-growing ants, and thief ants. The central idea seen throughout their food-gathering and food-storage habits and the spiritual analogies they teach is this: *It's all about nourishment!* Ants are divinely preprogrammed to diligently gather, store, share, maximize, and protect the substances and suppliers that nourish them. As a result of this blessed instinctive obsession, though they are very small, ants are very well fed. Millions of humans are starving today because of human-kind's persistently foolish laziness, wastefulness, greed, or lack of foresight. But not the ants; they are wise and industrious. They always have good food in their nests.

Army ants

Army ants differ from other ants in that they are blind, generally live above ground, do not store their food, and are fierce, relentless hunters. Rather than seek food only within close proximity to a fixed, central nest, large numbers (thousands to millions) of army ants march rapidly across the land in long, thin columns or ranks, swarming and, piece by tiny piece, eating whatever insects, spiders, or carrion they encounter. Remarkably, they are unhindered by their handicap of blindness. Sometimes they even swarm, kill, and eat very small animals that are unable to escape their sudden, overwhelming attacks. Of all species of ants, army ants are the most aggressive in their actions and warlike in their determination to obtain their food. For them, every day is Armageddon!

Like army ants, we Christians must *go to war* to nourish our souls. While not called to literal warfare or physical aggression, we are plainly summoned by Scripture to a spiritual war: "We do not war after the flesh (for the weapons of our warfare are not carnal, but mighty through God to the pulling down of strongholds)" (2 Cor. 10:3–4). In the Bible Jesus enjoined all of His followers to be violently resolute in our souls, ready to face the hardships that inevitably come our way when we set our faces to prayerfully seek and study His Word—our primary source of spiritual nourishment—on a regular basis and obey it in our daily living.

When He sent His first disciples to march through the land of Israel with His words, He plainly warned them that they would face the "sword" of spiritual division and conflict in their homes, just as He did in His. When briefing them for spiritual battle, He said:

> Think not that I am come to send peace on earth [in its present spiritual condition]; *I came not to send peace [first], but a sword [discord, division, war].*
>
> For I am come to set a [believing] man at variance against his [disbelieving or uncommitted] father, and the [ungodly] daughter against her [godly] mother. . . . And a man's foes [spiritual antagonists], shall be they of his own household [family].
> —MATTHEW 10:34–36

And John tells us that this was the case in Jesus' family:

> His brethren, therefore [knowing that "in
> Judea ... the Jews sought to kill him"], said unto
> him, Depart from here, and go into Judea, that thy
> disciples also may see the works that thou doest.
> For ... he himself seeketh to be known openly ...
> *for neither did his brethren believe in him.*
>
> —JOHN 7:1–5

Jesus further specified that His disciples would face varying degrees of tribulation, persecution, betrayal, and public rejection if they continued doing His will: "Beware of men; for they will deliver you up to the councils ... and ye shall be brought before governors and kings ... and the brother shall deliver up the brother ... and ye shall be hated of all men for my name's sake" (Matt. 10:17–23). Additionally, He warned that some of them would face violent opposition for His kingdom's sake: "From the days of John the Baptist until now the kingdom of heaven *suffereth violence*" (Matt. 11:12). And He taught that, in light of this, they should be as *forcefully determined* as soldiers in combat as they worked to enlarge His spiritual kingdom in their own souls and in others' in this hostile, satanically ruled society: "And *the violent* [forcefully determined] take it by force" (v. 12).

All Jesus' warnings apply to all "disciples indeed" in this Church Age. Church history soundly confirms this. All the original apostles except John died violent deaths for their faith and ministry. (The Romans cast John into a cauldron of boiling oil, but he survived, miraculously unharmed.[3]) From Pentecost to the present, every significant new release of kingdom truth, grace, and saving power and every new advance in the divine plan—groundbreaking vernacular Bible translations, key reformations of theology and faith, revivals of devotion and biblical methods, revelatory doctrines, visitations of the Holy Spirit—have elicited some form of hostile opposition from the disbelieving world and especially from backslidden church leaders.

Through the apostle Paul the Holy Spirit has called us to assume the resolute mentality of Christian soldiers: "Thou, therefore, endure hardness, as a *good soldier* of Jesus Christ" (2 Tim. 2:3). Only those disciples who have the wise, unrelenting determination of army ants will keep ranks and press through all opposition in order to continue nourishing their souls with the words of life when the forces of darkness continually oppose them. Paul fought this "good fight." "I have fought a *good fight*" (2 Tim. 4:7). Our "fight" is often over the places, channels, or means by which we receive spiritual nourishment: our Bible-expositing pastor; our biblically conformed church; our edifying weekly Bible study groups; our daily personal devotional reading; our morning or evening times of Bible study, prayer, and worship.

When Satan wars against us through his servants—by offenses, threats, distractions, temptations, reproaches, or rejections—are we ready to "put on the whole armor of God" (Eph. 6:11) and "stand fast" in our faith, not retaliating in the flesh, compromising God's Word, or succumbing to rebellion, impatience, or discouragement? And are we willing to endure *whatever* opposition comes, no matter how unreasonable, mean-spirited, or protracted, in order to retain our channels and means of spiritual nourishment?

Harvester ants

Most likely the species referred to in our proverbial text, harvester ants live in underground nests. They constantly collect seeds in the "summer" (Prov. 30:25), or warmer seasons of spring through autumn, and store them in seed chambers in their nests. When feeding, they break the seeds' hard outer husks and chew the inner kernels until they are a soft pulp known as "ant bread." They then squeeze the nutritious liquid out of the pulp and drink it. When wintertime visits, their nests are well stocked with an ample supply of seeds. As a result, harvester ants remain well fed and strong throughout winter, no matter how adverse the weather above ground.

Like harvester ants, we should steadily *gather, store, chew,* and *drink* spiritual nourishment, especially in the "summer" of our spiritual experience. Scripture teaches us repeatedly that God's Word is the seed of eternal life: "The seed is the word of God" (Luke 8:11). "Being born again, not of corruptible seed, but of incorruptible [seed], by the word of God" (1 Pet. 1:23). Hence we should gather *seeds of truth* regularly in daily Bible readings and ongoing Bible studies. And we should seek ministers who feed us seeds of biblical truth, not mere religious entertainment, excitement, popular trends, or trivia, and sit under their teaching regularly. When we find teaching resources that bless us—excellent devotionals, books, pamphlets, cassette tapes, tracts, DVDs, CDs, videos, and so forth—we should store, or retain, them in our personal libraries for future review and contemplation. As a rule, if any devotional or instructional material blesses us greatly, we should never discard it. Then, with antlike wisdom and efficiency, we may retrieve our seeds of truth and, by reviewing and meditating on them, "chew" them whenever they fit our current situational needs. As we do so, we will find them nourishing "word-bread" and will extract from them the sweet living water of the Holy Spirit, who fills God's words and every teaching that rightly divides them. Then we will not only endure, but also grow and thrive in, every wintertime of testing we meet, no matter how cold, dark, or long.

Admirably curious and intelligent though they were, the Athenian scholars erred by only desiring to hear "some new thing" (Acts 17:21). Realizing that God's truth is timeless, however, wise Christians seek both new and old seeds of truth. They learn to not only gather newly discovered seed-thoughts in their readings and Bible studies but also to revisit those that blessed them earlier. Just as Joseph wisely garnered Egypt's grain before its devastating famine, so these wise truth seekers habitually gather and store sound spiritual insights, teachings, and messages in the "summer," or initial, comparatively test- and stress-free season of their walk with God. Then, when the harsh demands of spiritual wintertime visit, they are ready to face the harder, longer trials of faith and patience God sends to mature them. Consequently, like harvester ants, they remain nourished and strong despite the spiritual coldness and danger surrounding them.

Are we gathering and storing nourishing seeds of biblical truth? Have we realized that our summer of opportunity is passing and our winter of trial drawing near? Or, if we're already in our wintertime of testing, are we revisiting our personal spiritual stores as needed and finding to our delight all the nourishment we need to continue thriving in our walk and work with God?

Dairying ants

Unlike harvesters, dairying ants subsist not on seeds but on a sugary liquid known as "honeydew," which they gather from plant lice, particularly aphids.

During warm months, aphids and other plant lice suck more sugary water from plant leaves than they need. When they release excess amounts of this honeydew, dairying ants, which visit the leaves solely for the honeydew, lick it up. They sometimes stroke the aphids with their antennae to induce them to release even more honeydew. Thus they "milk" the aphids of their honeydew. They also guard them. If other insects attack the aphids during this process, the ants drive them away. And, to ensure a continuing supply of honeydew, some dairying ants store plant lice eggs in their underground nests during the winter months. When the eggs hatch the following spring, they carry and place the newly hatched lice on plant leaves so they can begin producing honeydew—and so the ants can resume their seasonal nourishment cycle. Some dairying ants plant lice on underground roots that project into their nests, so the lice can continue feeding, growing, reproducing, and generating honeydew during the winter months. Just as dairy farmers raise herds of milk cows, so these ants raise growing "herds" of plant lice. Thus, the distinguishing feature of all dairying ants is that *they feed and protect those who feed them.* Why? So they can continue feeding off of them. In a sense, then, the ants and lice lovingly help each other survive on the sweetness of honeydew.

Incomparably sweet to those who love and live by it, the Word of God is the Christian's vital "honeydew." The psalmist said as much: "*How sweet are thy words* unto my taste! Yea, *sweeter than honey* to my mouth" (Ps. 119:103). The prophet Ezekiel agreed: "So I opened my mouth, and he caused me to eat that scroll [the word of God] . . . and it was in my mouth *like honey for sweetness*" (Ezek. 3:2–3). God's Word is especially sweet when, by the Spirit's help, it is fully explained and directly applied to our immediate pressing needs. The ecclesiastical "aphids" who release and supply us with this spiritual honeydew are ministers, most specifically our pastors and teachers. Scripture directs us to feed materially the servants of God who feed us spiritually. Consider these New Testament revelations and commands:

> Even so hath the Lord ordained that they who preach the gospel should live of the gospel.
> —1 CORINTHIANS 9:14

> Let the elders that rule well be counted worthy of double honor, especially they who labor in the word and doctrine. For the scripture saith, Thou shalt not muzzle the ox that treadeth out the grain; and, The laborer is worthy of his reward.
> —1 TIMOTHY 5:17–18, KJV

> Elders who do their work well should be paid well, especially those who work hard at both preaching and teaching. For the Scripture says, "Do not keep an ox from eating as it treads out the grain." And in another place, "Those who work deserve their pay!"
>
> —1 TIMOTHY 5:17–18, NLT

Because ministers are special targets of Satan's fury and plots, we should also stand by them when they come under attack for the sake of Christ and the ministry of His Word. By doing these things, we help those who help us—so they can continue helping us and so the whole body of Christ can grow vigorously.

Are we feeding with tithes and offerings the pastors and teachers who feed us, as the Philippians did for the apostle Paul? "Ye Philippians . . . ye sent once and again unto my necessity" (Phil. 4:15–16). Are we standing by them in their trials through loving communications and visitations, as Onesiphorus did for Paul? "Onesiphorus . . . he often refreshed me . . . in Rome, he sought me out very diligently, and found me" (2 Tim. 1:16–17). Are we also helping them through persisting intercession in the Spirit, as the believers in Jerusalem did for Peter? "Peter . . . was kept in prison; but prayer was made without ceasing by the church unto God for him" (Acts 12:5). Or are we abandoning them in their valleys of sorrow, as many Christians did Paul? "At my first defense no man stood with me, but all men forsook me" (2 Tim. 4:16). If we are as wise as dairying ants, we will help those who help us—so they can continue helping us, and, together, all of us can thrive in God's will. This is the Spirit and Scripture's vision for the church: "The whole body . . . by that which every joint supplieth . . . maketh increase of the body unto the edifying of itself in love" (Eph. 4:16).

Honey ants

Honey (or honeypot) ants gather sugar water from both plants and insects during the warm months and store it in their nests in a most unusual way. These worker ants "feed" (by regurgitation) the liquid they have gathered to other worker ants called "repletes," who serve, as one source put it, as "living storage tanks" for the entire colony. As the repletes take in the honeydew, their gasters expand significantly. Eventually they become so large they can hardly move, so they simply hang, virtually motionless, from the tops of their nest chambers. When their fellow ants wish to receive nourishment, they touch the repletes with their antennae. This prompts the repletes to release honeydew (by regurgitation) for them.

Just as repletes are exceptionally full of honeydew, so *ministers are called to be extraordinarily filled, or replete, with spiritual "honeydew"—the sweet, nourishing, and timely knowledge of God*. Ideally, pastors, teachers, elders, and counselors should be living repositories of spiritual knowledge readily accessible to every Christian who thirsts to know God better. When "touched" by their questions, or when delivering teachings or sermons (composed of pre-viously digested spiritual truths), ministers should release nourishing words that comfort, convict, deliver, explain, or guide: "For the priest's [or minister's] lips should keep knowledge, and *they [God's people] should seek the law at his mouth*; for he is the messenger of the LORD of hosts" (Mal. 2:7).

Apollos was one of God's repletes. "Mighty in the scriptures," he helped the Christians of Corinth "much" (Acts 18:24, 27). Paul was another exceptionally filled with vital biblical and revelatory knowledge. He released much spiritual honeydew through his epistles: "*Paul*, also according to the wisdom given unto him *hath written unto you*" (2 Pet. 3:15). King Solomon was arguably the greatest "living storage tank" of God's wisdom ever: "And God gave Solomon wisdom and very much understanding, and largeness of heart. . . . And Solomon's wisdom excelled the wisdom of all the children of the east" (1 Kings 4:29–30). The Lord told Solomon explicitly, "There was none like thee [in wisdom and understanding of heart] before thee, *neither after thee shall any arise like unto thee*" (1 Kings 3:12). Solomon released his honeydew primarily through the numerous proverbs he recited regularly to the gatherings of courtiers, royals, and sages who eagerly sought his wisdom: "And he spoke three thousand proverbs . . . and there came from all peoples to hear the wisdom of Solomon" (1 Kings 4:32–34). He also released a significant amount of it through his inspired canonical writings, including the Book of Proverbs, Ecclesiastes, and the Song of Solomon.

Where are our ministerial repletes today? Admittedly, the sedentary, privileged positions most pastors and teachers enjoy tend to swell our heads or midriffs—or both. But where are those aspiring or practicing ministers, who, wholly dedicated to the pursuit of spiritual knowledge, are filling their *hearts* daily with an unusually large volume of timely biblical insights? Whoever and wherever these ministers are, they have this in common: they are shut away with God in their private study chambers a significant part of every day, prayerfully seeking and drinking in sweet insights, energizing revelations, and refreshing messages. Without exception, ministers who have blessed the church exceptionally have given themselves to exceptionally deep, sustained, private Bible study, devotional and other reading, and prayer. That is the hidden "underground chamber" in which they have discovered and stored all the sweet, living waters with which they have refreshed us.

Wisely, these ministerial repletes have taken Paul's instructions to Timothy as their own: "Till I come, give attendance to reading . . . meditate upon these things; *give thyself wholly to them*" (1 Tim. 4:13, 15). They have also followed the pattern of the church's original repletes, the apostles, who wisely decided: "*We will give ourselves continually to prayer, and to the ministry of the word*" (Acts 6:4). Consequently, they allow nothing and no one to distract them from their primary call to constantly drink, digest, and share sweet Bible truths. Every divinely ordained minister dispenses spiritual honeydew, but ministerial repletes are unusually full of the sweet truths of God. Every time we read or listen to them, we get an exceptionally rich, nourishing, and satisfying taste of heavenly honey!

Fungus-growing ants

Fungus-growing ants, which are found only in North and South America, are diligent subterranean gardeners. They cultivate various kinds of fungi (simple non-green plants without roots, stems, and leaves, such as molds, mildews, and mushrooms) in special chambers in their underground nests designated as "gardens." These fungi produce nourishing "knobs" (ant "mushrooms," if you please), on which the ants feed and subsist. Fungus growers continually gather loose fragments of leaves, flower petals, and other plant materials, carry them down into their nests, chew them to a pulp, and place the pulp on their fungus gardens to fertilize them. Some of these ants, the "leaf cutters," cut pieces of living tree and plant leaves for the same purpose. So large and efficient are some of their colonies in South America that they have been known to completely strip an orange orchard of its leaves in a single night! All the assiduous labors of fungus-growing ants are aimed at cultivating—or developing growth and improving productivity by steady attention and labor—their hidden fungus gardens. In a word, they are *efficient cultivators* of their nourishment resources.

As Christians, we know that our prime spiritual nourishment resource is the Word of God. With it, we live and prosper; without it, we die. The more divine words we "eat," the stronger we are. Jesus declared, "Man shall not live by [eating] bread alone, but by [eating] every word of God" (Luke 4:4). He also called us to continuously and systematically build our knowledge of God's Word: "If ye continue in [study of and obedience to] my word, then are ye my disciples indeed; and ye shall know the truth, and the truth shall make you free" (John 8:31–32). If we are as wise as fungus-growing ants, we will *efficiently cultivate* the "garden" of the knowledge of God that lies beneath the surface of our lives, deep down in the hidden chambers of our inner man.

To do so, we must begin by honestly assessing our present "garden" of biblical knowledge. Which "plants," or categories of Bible truth, are we strong in? Which are we weak in and, as a result, need our cultivating: The Gospels? The Epistles? Old Testament history? New Testament history? The wisdom and poetical books? The prophets? The apocalyptic writings? After assessing our deficiencies, we should begin reading and studying in the areas in which we are weak. We should also gather new "leaf cuttings," or pieces, of valuable spiritual knowledge wherever we find them—in meetings, books, magazines, broadcasts, conversations, and seminars, so we can fertilize, and thus increase, our garden of biblical knowledge.

Too often Christians develop a favorite theological or doctrinal "plant"—the Second Coming, prophecy, healing, the baptism with the Holy Spirit, the gifts of the Spirit, prosperity, revival, prayer, etc. They read, study, and listen to teaching *only* if it fertilizes their "pet plant." As a result, one part of their heart-garden thrives, while other areas remain dry, withered, and fruitless. Why? They are not making a sustained, conscious effort to cultivate a broader knowledge of biblical truth. They are true Christians, all right, but poor spiritual gardeners.

Acutely aware of this danger, the apostle Paul steadily cultivated a broad knowledge of God's Word in his heart. He then fed himself and others from the verdant spiritual vegetation and fruit that grew in his full, rich, soul garden. At Miletus, Paul reminded the Ephesian elders that, at one time or another, they had feasted on all his healthful theological "veggies." "I have not shunned to declare unto you *all the counsel of God*" (Acts 20:27). He then advised all of them—and everyone in ministry today!—to follow his example: "*Take heed, therefore, unto yourselves . . . to feed the church of God [with the 'whole counsel of God']*" (v. 28). Are we heeding his wise counsel?

Are we efficiently cultivating a rich, full garden of the knowledge of God in our souls? Or are we continually watering only one area of doctrine? Our response to this probe will either allow or disallow the Spirit to fulfill Isaiah's prophecy in us: "And thou [your soul] shalt be like a watered garden" (Isa. 58:11). It will also reveal if we have the wisdom of an ant.

Thief ants

Succinctly, thief ants are *outrageous opportunists*. By whatever passageways are open, these little fellows invade houses, restaurants, or any other buildings with food stores, and, with the audacity and conscience of a thief, simply take and eat whatever they can find! And they continue shamelessly eating, eating, eating, until they are stopped by human inhabitants or insecticides! Their low-life constitution reads, "As long as your door is open, we'll walk through it. If your food is accessible, it's ours. Your inattention is our invitation, and your loss, our gain." Outstanding citizens, they are not; outrageous opportunists, they are!

Just as one of Jesus' parables commends an unjust steward's *foresight* but not his altering of his master's accounts (Luke 16:1–9), so we should emulate the thief ant's *opportunism* but not his thievery. Simply put, we should become *outstanding opportunists*. That is, *we should avail ourselves of every opportunity for spiritual edification, growth, and development.* Let me explain.

If there is a Christ-centered, New Testament church near us, we should join it. If there are excellent Bible teachers nearby, we should sit under their ministries. If we know of Spirit-filled, God-honoring prayer meetings, we should attend them. If we discover a godly Christian counselor, we should seek God's counsel from him or her as needed. When outstanding men or women of God visit our area, we should attend their meetings. If we discover spiritually potent Christian magazines or e-mailings, we should subscribe. If we find edifying, regularly updated Web sites, we should visit them periodically. When we learn of exceptionally God-focused camp meetings, retreats, conferences, or seminars, we should attend them if at all possible. When we find very informational, inspirational, or insightful books, we should buy and devour them. When certain radio or television ministries consistently bless us, we should take in their broadcasts regularly. And we should continue consuming all the spiritual food we find in these resources until God closes these doors of blessing or moves us to a different "nest." By thus maximizing our opportunities to nourish our souls we become *outstanding opportunists*—and replicate the wisdom, though not the unlawful temerity, of thief ants.

Are we taking full advantage of our opportunities for spiritual edification? Or are we failing to walk through the inviting doors of inspiration God has graciously opened before us?

No wonder Solomon and Agur were impressed with the "exceedingly wise" ant! I'm taken aback—and embarrassed. Why? Because I used to believe that humans, particularly redeemed ones, were God's wisest creatures, but my overly inflated, self-congratulatory confidence in human wisdom has taken a serious and terminal hit. I now fear that the wisest creatures may live far beneath us. Why?

Because the ants are so sharp! Are we reading, writing, thinking, and so increasing our mental sharpness? The ants are so industrious! Are we steadily and persistently working to accomplish God's will? The ants are so completely under authority! Do we respect and obey our "queens" or despise, circumvent, or mock our authorities? The ants are so highly organized! Are our home "nests" and church "colonies" well ordered and functioning smoothly? The ants are so resolutely determined! Are we so committed to Jesus that we're willing to wage spiritual warfare when necessary? The ants are so highly interdependent! Are we lovingly communicating with and exhorting one another daily in our church "colonies"? And, most importantly, every day the ants so truly live and demonstrate their unofficial motto: *It's all about nourishment!* Are we equally convinced we *must* have spiritual nourishment? Are we living and demonstrating this inspired conviction? That is, are we seriously gathering, storing, sharing, supporting, protecting, and maximizing our sources of spiritual edification?

Now we have obeyed God. As instructed, we have gone to the ant and considered her ways. And, indeed, her ways are wise, wiser than many of ours—and that despite the ant having a brain weighing one-millionth what ours does![4] There's only one thing left to do: Step out of our ways and into the wise ways of ants. May every believer do so, and soon! Why?

Because, frankly, it would be eternally embarrassing if at last the angels were forced to write of our generation of Christians: "There was more wisdom in the house of the ants than in the house of the saints!"

NOTES

Chapter 1: Making Vessels of Honor

1. Seagrove Area Potters Association (SAPA), Web site: http://www.discoverseagrove.com (accessed September 21, 2006).
2. North Carolina Pottery Center, 250 East Avenue, Seagrove, NC 27341. Telephone (336) 873-8430. E-mail: NCPC@atomic.net. Web site: www.ncpotterycenter.com (accessed September 21, 2006).
3. Turn and Burn Pottery, 124 East Avenue, P.O. Box 371, Seagrove, NC 27341. Telephone (336) 873-7381. E-mail: dbgarner1@earthlink.net. Web site: http://www.turnandburnpottery.com (accessed September 21, 2006).
4. "Just As I Am" by Charlotte Elliott. Public domain.

Chapter 2: The Ways of Eagle Christians

1. Unless otherwise noted, all information concerning eagles has been taken from the *World Book Encyclopedia* (Chicago, IL: 1980). Also, the *World Book Encyclopedia* (Chicago, IL: 2003).
2. Edwin Way Teale, "Bird of Freedom," *Atlantic Monthly*, 1957, referenced in Rebecca L. Grambo, editor, *Eagles: Masters of the Sky* (Stillwater, MN: Voyageur Press, 1997).
3. "Migration of Birds," Northern Prairie Wildlife Research Center, U.S. Geological Survey, http://www.npwrc.usgs.gov/resource/birds/migratio/altitude.htm (accessed September 21, 2006).
4. "American Bald Eagle Description," BaldEagleInfo.com, http://

www.baldeagleinfo.com/eagle/eagle-facts.html (accessed December 4, 2006). Also, Rebecca L. Grambo, editor, *Eagles: Masters of the Sky.*

5. "Raptor Species: Golden Eagle," Carolina Raptor Center, Carolinaraptorcenter.org, http://www.carolinaraptorcenter. org/g_eagle.php (accessed September 22, 2006).

6. Frances Hamerstrom, *An Eagle to the Sky* (Guilford, CT: Lyons Press, 1970).

7. "American Bald Eagle Information," Baldeagleinfo.com, http://www.baldeagleinfo.com/eagle/eagle4.html (accessed December 6, 2006).

8. "American Bald Eagle Information," Baldeagleinfo.com, http://www.baldeagleinfo.com/eagle/eagle8.html (accessed September 22, 2006).

9. For additional information on eagles: Noel and Helen Snyder, *Raptors of North America* (St. Paul, MN: Voyageur Press, 2006) and Candace Savage, *Eagles of North America* (Vancouver, BC: Greystone Books, 1987).

Chapter 3: The Salt of the Earth

1. Unless otherwise noted, all information in this chapter regarding the composition, location, methods of extraction, and historic and modern uses of salt has been taken from the *World Book Encyclopedia* (Chicago, IL, 1980). Also, the *World Book Encyclopedia* (Chicago, IL: 2003).

2. *Food Chemicals Codex*, Fourth Edition (Washington DC: National Academy Press, 1996).

3. *Wycliffe Bible Encyclopedia* (Chicago, IL: Moody Press, 1975).

4. *Zondervan Pictorial Bible Dictionary* (Grand Rapids, MI: Zondervan Publishing House, 1967).

5. For additional information, see the Web site of the Salt Institute, http://www.saltinstitute.org (accessed September 21, 2006).

6. Unpublished annotations of Walter F. Beuttler, "The Offerings," page 4. Public domain.

Chapter 5: The Wise Ways of Ants

1. Unless otherwise noted, all information in this chapter regarding ants has been taken from the *World Book Encyclopedia* (Chicago, IL: 1980). Also, the *World Book Encyclopedia* (Chicago, IL: 2003).
2. Edward O. Wilson, "Ants: The Civilized Insect," *National Geographic*, vol. 210, no. 2, August 2006.
3. John Foxe, *Foxe's Book of Martyrs* (Peabody, MA: Hendrickson Publishers, 2004).
4. Wilson, "Ants: The Civilized Insect."

OTHER BOOKS BY THIS AUTHOR

Walking in His Ways

Walking on Water

Daniel Notes: An Inspirational Commentary on the Book of Daniel

Precious Pearls From the Proverbs

Key New Testament Passages on Divorce and Remarriage

Spiritual Truths for Overcoming Adversity

About This Ministry . . .

Mission Statement

GREG HINNANT MINISTRIES exists to train believers to walk in New Testament discipleship by teaching the timeless, priceless, and unfailing principles of the Word of God. In this way we are contributing to the spiritual preparation of the bride of Christ in anticipation of the appearing of Jesus Christ.

Our slogan is, "Prepare ye the way of the LORD" (Isa. 40:3).

Ministries Available

We presently offer a free *weekly devotional* (e-mail only) and a free *monthly Bible message* (preferably e-mail or by hard copy) to interested believers. To subscribe to these mailings, or browse the books, cassette tapes, and CDs we offer for sale, please visit our Web site at: www.greghinnantministries.org. Or you may contact us directly.

To Contact This Ministry

Mail:	Greg Hinnant Ministries
	P. O. Box 788
	High Point, NC 27261
Telephone:	(336) 882-1645
Fax:	(336) 886-7227
E-mail:	rghministries@aol.com